FULL SALVATION

FULL SALVATION
GOD'S GRACE, PROMISES AND EXPECTATIONS

BY Dr. Richard T. Hise

XULON PRESS

Xulon Press
2301 Lucien Way #415
Maitland, FL 32751
407.339.4217
www.xulonpress.com

Unless otherwise indicated, Scripture quotations taken from the Holy Bible, New International Version (NIV). Copyright © 1973, 1978, 1984, 2011 by Biblica, Inc.™. Used by permission. All rights reserved.

Scripture quotations taken from King James version (KJV), Zondervan Publishing Co., Grand Rapids, MI, 2092.Printed in the United States of America.

ISBN-13: 9781545641729

CHAPTER ONE

INTRODUCTION

"For God hath not appointed us to wrath, but to obtain salvation by our Lord Jesus Christ." (1 Thessalonians 5:9).

WHAT IS THE MOST IMPORTANT DECISION that you will ever make? Common responses are "Who will I marry?" "Should I and my spouse have children?" "What college or university should I attend?" "What major should I choose?" "What career path should I follow?" "Where should I live?" And there are probably dozens of others that could have been included. No matter what you will put on your list, they all pale in comparison to where you will spend eternity.

Scoffers will evade dealing with this question by stating that it is a non-starter because there is no heaven or hell or that there is not even a God. The scoffers are wrong on all counts.

One only has to look at nature to conclude that there is a God. Trees, grasses, animals, fish, birds, fruits, vegetables, lakes, rivers, mountains, valleys, seas and oceans, stones, rocks, gold, silver, gem stones, day and night, all proclaim the existence of God. And let's not forget humans, perhaps His greatest creation. Consider the miraculous bodies that we humans have: eyes to see, ears to hear, noses with which to smell, thumbs to facilitate grasping, legs that allow us to walk and run, lungs that enable us to breathe, hearts that pump and circulate blood, kidneys to circulate it, and so on. Some medical experts have said that our bodies are so remarkable that we could easily live for 150 years—if we took better care of ourselves.

Of course, evolutionists maintain that humans were not created but that we evolved over thousands of years from the lowest class of being existing initially in some dark, murky, smelly swamp. What bunk! Of course, the major reason why evolutionists deny the existence of God is that they do not want to subject themselves to a higher authority: they want to be free to do what they want to do, when they want to do it, and where they want to do it. In other words, they want to sin and not be subjected to any repercussions.

Unfortunately, God hates sin. Adam and Eve were created sinless. As such, they were told that they could do anything in the Garden of Eden except eat of the tree of knowledge of good and evil. Eve, beguiled by Satan (in the form of a serpent) and Adam, at the urging of Eve, ate the forbidden fruit whereupon sin entered the world, graphically illustrated by Adam and Eve hiding from God because they then believed that nakedness was a sin.

When God's son, Jesus Christ, was hanging on the cross, he uttered: "My God, my God, why hast thou forsaken me?" (Matthew 27:46). Bible scholars believe that Jesus had seen His Heavenly Father turn away from Him because all of the sins that everyone who has ever lived, is living, or who would ever live, were heaped upon Jesus, and God could not stand to see such immorality.

Except for Jesus Christ, all people have sinned. Romans 3:23 is often cited in support of this principle. The apostle Paul says: "For all have sinned and come short of the glory of God." The ultimate penalty for sin is death, that is, separation from God. Recall that as punishment for Adam and Eve's sin, they were banished (separated from God) from the garden of Eden. They, thus, no longer had a personal relationship with God.

Because God is also a loving God, He decided to provide sinful mankind with one, and only one, way to escape death and be granted eternal life (salvation): He sent Jesus Christ to die for our sins, thus satisfying God's dissatisfaction with sin. John 14:6 is perhaps the proof text for God's solution for our sins: "I am the way, the truth and the life: no man comes unto the Father but by me" (Jesus' words).

Some years ago, I watched Franklin Graham, Billy Graham's son, being interviewed by Larry King. King asked Graham how a person could achieve eternal life. Graham's reply was to quote John 14:6. King then asked Graham if various high profile people, including some who were not Christains but were universrally recognized as "good people," would be granted salvation. In each case, Mr. Graham repeated John 14:6.

In addition to being separated from God, unsaved persons will be consigned to Hell. For those individuals who do not believe that there is a Hell (or Hades or Sheol), be advised that Jesus referred to Hell 16 items in the New Testament. Some of these verses include:"

1. "And if thy right eye offend thee, puck it out and cast it from thee: for it is profitable for thee that one of thy members should perish, and not the whole body should be cast into Hell" (Matthew 5:29).
2. Ye serpents, ye generation of vipers, how can ye all escape the damnation of Hell? (Matthew 23:33).
3. "I am He that liveth and was dead; and behold, I am alive for evermore, amen: and have the keys of Hell and of death (Jesus' words, Revelation 1:18).

Some Biblical passages indicate the nature of punishment in Hell that awaits the unsaved. These include fire (Matthew 5:22, Matthew 18:9, Mark 9:45, and Mark 9:47), destruction of body and soul (Matthew 10:28), damnation (Matthew 23:33) and torment, flame, thirst, a great gulf between those in Hell and those not in Hell (story of the rich man and Lazarus, as told by Jesus) (Luke 16:19-26).

Some people point to God's love and patience with man as support for the belief that there is no such place as Hell and even if there is, sinners will only be there temporarily before joining Jesus in Heaven. Those who subscribe to these suppositions ignore the fact that there is another dimension of God: He is also a God of wrath (or anger or fury). There are about 180 references in the

Bible to God's anger, 60 to His fury and 130 to His wrath. (See Strong's Exhaustive Concordance of the Bible).

What aspects of God's wrath can be gleaned from an examination of these passages?

These are:

1. Because God is sovereign, his wrath is always justified.
2. His anger is always under control.
3. His anger and the subsequent punishment are appropriate for the sins committed.
4. The punishment meted out by God because of his anger can be accomplished through people or through natural events.
5. His anger will be satisfied when justice has been fully carried out (Aid To Bible Understanding).
6. God's anger often results from false worship on the part of His people when they turn to other gods—as Israel often did.
7. His wrath can be provoked by actions directed against His chosen people. Example; in the prophetic book of Ezekiel, here is His reaction to a future invasion of Israel by Iran, Russia, Libya, and other nations.: "...that my fury will come up in my face." He then proceeds to destroy five sixths of this invading army)
8. God's anger may be delayed. Joel 2:13 states: "And turn unto the Lord your God: For He is gracious and merciful, slow to anger, and of great kindness."
9. God's anger may be avoided through the repentance of a supplicant. In 2 Chronicles 29:10, King Hezekiah pleads: "Now it is in my heart to make a covenant with the Lord God of Israel that his fierce wrath may turn away from us." In 1 Thessalonians 1:10, we read: "And to wait for His Son from heaven, whom he raised from the dead even Jesus: Which delivered us from the wrath to come." Some Biblical experts believe this passage refers to the saved not having to endure the Great Tribulation because they will have been taken up to Heaven via the Rapture before the Great Tribulation begins.

10. God's anger may be shortened. Micah 7:18 says: "He retaineth not His anger forever because he delighteth in mercy."

The sheer magnitude of mentions of Heaven in the Bible supports the contention that there is a place called Heaven in the Bible, 320 in the Old Testament and 250 in the New Testament. Heaven is mentioned 114 times by Jesus.

Many people who are not saved believe that they can obtain eternal life in Heaven through works. This fallacious thinking has sent many people to Hell. Ephesians 2: 8-9 states: "For by grace are ye saved through faith, and that not of yourselves: it is the gift of God: NOT OF WORKS, lest any man should boast" (emphasis added). (This passage is believed to be the catalyst for Martin Luther's break with the Catholic Church that jump started the Reformation).

Jesus warns us not to be taken in by false prophets or false christs who perform wondrous works, such as, casting out devils and performing great signs and wonders (Matthew 7:22 and Mark 13:22). Jesus dismisses the doers of these works by saying: "...I never knew you: depart from me that work iniquity (Matthew 7:23).

This book will discuss salvation as a process, not as a one-time event. This process is captured in a general sense in Exhibit 1. Each will be discussed in detail in subsequent chapters.

EXHIBIT 1.1
THE SALVATION PROCESS

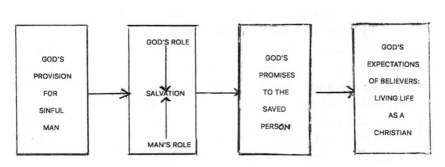

The objectives of this book are to (1) emphasize the need for people to receive salvation; (2) indicate how this is accomplished; (3) identify the various components of salvation; (4) reveal the promises that God has made to those who are saved; (5) provide God's template as to how Christians need to live before they are called home; (6) enhance your understanding of your conversion, especially if you are a new Christian; (7) enable you to do a more effective job of witnessing to the unsaved; and (8) introduce the reader, in simplified terms, to important aspects of salvation that most Christians do not really understand.

The author used a variety of sources in writing this book. By far the most important is the Bible. I prefer the King James Study Bible (see references) because I am more familiar with its wording, as compared to more recent versions, and the numerous accompanying notes are most helpful.

The most important reason for relying heavily on the Bible is that it contains the inerrant words of God. Josh McDowell, in his book, God Breathed, develops a compelling case for the inerrancy of the Bible. He first cites various passages from the scriptures, such as, Matthew 5:18: "For verily I say unto you, Till heaven and earth pass, one jot or one tittle shall in no wise pass from the law till all be fulfilled." He uses three tests to substantiate the validity of the Bible. These are the bibliographical test ("determining whether the text of the historical record has been transmitted accurately"), the external evidence test ("determining whether the historical record has been affirmed by data outside itself") and the internal evidence test ("determined how the historical record stands up to the test of internal validity").

I also used several Biblical references, including Bible dictionaries, encyclopedias, and concordances (see references).

I examined over 400 hymns (see references). The rationale is that these hymns were composed by born again individuals so it would be rewarding to see how well their lyrics support the aspects of salvation presented in this book. Many of these hymns emphasize three major themes: the Christian as a sinner before salvation, salvation, and the Christian's life after being saved. Some hymns addressed two or even all three of these themes.

6

The author also included some hymns that could be rightly called "secular hymns." Examples include "He," "I Believe," and "Count Your Many Blessings."

An added benefit for the reader of including an analysis of hymns is that he or she will be introduced to some of history's outstanding Christians. These include Marin Luther, Fanny Crosby, Charles Wesley, Isaac Watts, Ira Sankey, Charles Moody, Julia Ward Howe, Felix Mendelsohn, Franz Gruber, Charles Gabriel, John Newton, Robert Schumann, and Henry Wadsworth Longfellow.

In preparation to write this book, I twice went through the New Testament verse by verse. I also drew on my 50+ years of intense, albeit some times sporadic, study of the Bible, as well as consulting appropriate reference sources and works by various Christian authors.

The reader will undoubtedly notice that this is a relatively short book. I purposely kept it brief because I wanted to attract readers, stimulate their interest, and not overwhelm them with a lot of esoteric, pedantic material.

CHAPTER TWO

GOD'S PROVISION FOR SINFUL MAN

"…for I am not come to call the righteous but sinners to repentance" (Matthew 9:13)

B ECAUSE GOD IS A GOD OF LOVE, HE DECIDED to provide a way for mankind to avoid the penalty for sinning, that is, the consignment of their souls to Hell for eternity. This way out would result from His son, Jesus Christ, being sent to Earth to die on the cross instead of us. Jesus, himself, said "….for I am not come to call the righteous but sinners to repentance" (Matthew 9:13).

WHO CAN BE SAVED?

It is important to understand that this "escape hatch" is available to EVERYONE, regardless of their age, ethnicity, gender, where they live, even the multitude and severity of their sins—as long as they have accepted Jesus Christ as their Lord and savior. In Acts 4:12, the apostle Peter said: "Neither is there salvation in any other: for there is none other name under Heaven given among men, whereby we must be saved." John 3:16-17 states: "For God so loved the world that he gave his only begotten Son, that

WHOSOEVER believeth in Him should not perish, but have everlasting life. For God sent not his Son into the world to condemn the world: but that the WORLD through Him might be saved." 1 Timothy 2:3-4 echoes this sentiment: "For this is good and acceptable in the sight of God our Savior; Who will have ALL MEN to be saved...."Peter said (Acts 10:34-35) "of a truth I perceive that God is NO RESPECTER OF PERSONS: But in every nation that heareth Him and worketh righteousness, is accepted with Him." The note accompanying this verse says: "God DOES NOT favor an individual because of his station in life, his nationality or his material possessions." Corroborating scriptures are found in James 2:1, Romans 2:11, Ephesians 6:9, and Colossians 3:25. (The above emphases were provided by the author).

There are no scriptures that better demonstrate God's desire that all be saved than Luke 15:7-8: "I say unto you that likewise joy shall be in heaven over all sinners who repenteth."

A major schism among Christian Jews after the death and resurrection of Jesus was whether Gentiles (non-Jews) could also receive salvation. This question was decided in the affirmative by Peter when he witnessed to Cornelius, a Roman centurion, and others.

Gentiles and they received Jesus Christ as their savior, whereupon the Holy Spirit fell upon them. Acts 11:18 states: "...then hath God also to the Gentiles granted repentance unto life" (a statement of agreement by Jewish Christians who had heretofore believed that salvation was only available to the Jews).

After Paul's conversion on the road to Damascus, Ananias, a disciple of Jesus', was instructed to go to Paul and restore his sight. When Ananias voiced reluctance, God said to him: "Go thy way; for he is a chosen vessel unto me, to bear my name before the GENTILES, and kings, and the children of Israel" (Acts 9:15), Emphasis is added. If God did not intend to offer salvation to the Gentiles, it is unlikely that He would have spoken these words to Ananias.

Another indication that salvation was also available for Gentiles is found in Acts 14:11 when Paul and Barnabas preached in the synagogue in Liconium when "a great multitude both of the Jews and also of the Greeks believed."

9

WILL GOD DENY SALVATION TO PEOPLE
WHO COMMIT GRIEVOUS SINS?

Many people believe, falsely, that their sins are so grievous (and so numerous) that God will never forgive them, they will not be saved, and will, as a result, be consigned forever to Hell. The life of a prominent, sin-laden person in the Bible, Paul (formerly called Saul), emphatically refutes this notion. Here is why, after his conversion, Paul referred to himself as the "chief sinner" (1 Timothy 1:15):

1. He approved the stoning of Stephen, the first Christian martyr.
2. He was an active participant in this act since he held the garments of those who did the actual stoning.
3. He viciously persecuted the early Christians.
4. When a decision had to be made as to whether Christians should be killed, he voted affirmatively.
5. He tried to get Christians to recant their faith.
6. He had Christians thrown into prison.
7. He persecuted Christians outside of Jerusalem.
8. He was authorized to go Damascus to seek out Christians and bring them to Jerusalem for trial (Aid to Bible Understanding).

Some years ago, on a Sunday, I was driving my car and listening to The Lutheran Hour on the radio. The speaker was discussing the fate of the top Nazis who participated in the killing of six million Jews and three million other "undesirables:" Gypsies, homosexuals, Jehovah's Witnesses, Communists, political opponents and other dissidents, Catholic priests, Protestant ministers, etc). The top 21 Nazi leaders were tried at Nuremburg. The list included some of the most evil and sadistic men who have ever lived, including Hans Frank (governor-general of Poland), Wilhelm Frick (minister of the interior), Alfred Jodl (chief of the German high command), Ernst Kaltenbrunner (head of the Gestapo and the SD), Wilhelm Keitel (chief of staff, German high command), Joachim von Ribbentrop (foreign minister), Alfred Rosenberg (head, Eastern occupied territories), Arthur Seys-Inquart (commissioner of the Netherlands),

Albert Speer (head of armament and munitions), Julius Streicher (anti-semitic editor), and Herman Goering (commander of the German Air Force). About half of the defendants were sentenced to death by hanging or life in prison.

The announcer indicated that some of the defendants made a profession of faith in Jesus Christ before or after their sentencing. He went on to say that many of the listeners to the program would be shocked by this revelation but essentially said that they had no right to question God's plan of salvation and who would be saved. (God, himself, essentially said the same thing to Jonah when this minor prophet became angry that, through his preaching, the city of Nineveh was spared God's wrath because the inhabitants had repented of their sins).

WHAT ABOUT THE LAW AND SALVATION?

The standard of behavior that determined a Jew's standing before God prior to the coming of Jesus Christ was how well they observed the law. The corner stone of the law was, of course, the Ten Commandments (Exodus 20:17). But, in addition to the Ten Commandments, God, Israel's kings, and the nation's priests and rabbis formulated thousands of other dos and donts that pertained to all aspects of Jewish life. The Aid To Bible Understanding lists the Old Testament laws that applied to the following areas: civil government, the military, judicial system, criminal law, marriage, parent-children relationships, real property, individual conduct and duties, sanitary and dietary laws, and business practices. In total, I counted about 350 specific laws within these 10 categories.

When Jesus Christ came to earth, the paradigm through which people could relate to God was changed. John 14:6 is illustrative: "I am the way, the truth, and the life: no man comet unto the Father but by me." Luke 16:16 says: "The law and the prophets were until John: since that time the kingdom of God is preached and every man presseth into it." The note on this passage says that "The ministry of John the Baptist, which prepared the way for Jesus the Messiah, was the dividing line between the OT (the law and the prophets) and the NT." Hebrews 8:8 says "Behold the days come, saith the

11

Lord, when I will make a new covenant with the house of Israel and with the house of Juda." 2 Timothy 1:9 clearly indicates that works (adhering to the law) do not save: "Who hath saved us and called us with a holy calling, NOT according to our works, but according to his own purpose and GRACE, which was given to us in Jesus Christ BEFORE THE WORLD BEGAN" (emphases added).

The point that needs to be made is that works no longer have any relevance as to whether someone is saved. The litmus test is has that person accepted Jesus Christ as his or her lord and savior? Works do have an important role in Christians' lives—after they have been saved. This topic will be discussed in Chapter Six.

THE ROLE OF THE HOLY SPIRIT IN SALVATION

Besides God and Jesus Christ, there is another being that is an important and necessary participant in the process of salvation. This supernatural being is the third part of the holy trinity, the Holy Spirit.

What role does the Spirit play in bringing men and women to Jesus? (We will see in Chapter Six how the Spirit works with and through saved individuals). The note on 2 Corinthians 3:17—" and where the Spirit of the Lord is, there is liberty"—states"… the first two persons of the trinity accomplished their purposes through the Spirit." Thus, since God and Jesus want all mankind to be saved, it must be that, through the workings of the Holy Spirit, men and women are brought to a saving knowledge of Jesus Christ. In interpreting Romans 8:11, 16-17, Nelson's New Illustrated Bible Dictionary states: "The Holy Spirit is the way to Jesus Christ the Son and to the Father." This same source says that the Holy Spirit is "the person who bears witness to us that we are the children of God (Romans 8:16-17) and that it is through the Holy Spirit that "one confesses that Jesus is Lord" (1 Corinthians 12:3)

Hebrews 3:7-8 says"…Today if ye will hear his voice, harden not your hearts…." This passage suggests that when the Holy Spirit calls, a person should heed the call. A similar warning occurs in 2 Corinthians 6:2: "…now is the accepted time; behold, now is the day of salvation." The hymn, "I Will Praise Him (Harris/Harris) nicely captures the Holy Spirit's role in salvation: "I obeyed the Spirit's wooing when He said wilt thou be clean?"

WHY DO PEOPLE BECOME SAVED?

What are the internal and external factors or stimuli that figure in an individual becoming saved? (In chapters Three and Four, the various components of salvation itself will be discussed).

INTERNAL FACTORS

Some people are saved because they have reached such a low point in their lives that they have nowhere to turn except to Jesus Christ. They may be deep in sin, an alcoholic, a drug addict, an adulterer, into pornography, an abuser, destitute, and so on. They may have tried to extricate themselves from these entrapments but realize that they can't do so on their own. At the end of their rope, in desperation, they call upon Jesus Christ to pull them out of the quagmire.

There is a program that airs on many Christian radio stations and is produced by Pacific Garden Mission in Chicago. It is called "Unshackled" and it presents true stories of people, often men who were alcoholics, who in desperation called on Jesus for help, and through the power of salvation, became sober and often productive Christians for the balance of their lives.

Poor health may be the catalyst for people being saved. Doctors have not been able to cure them—they feel that death is imminent— and they reach out to the Lord for help and are saved.

Some people are saved because they realize that their lives have been meaningless. This happened to a colleague and close friend of mine who decided that making lots of money and having expensive cars and a palatial home were no longer important to him. After his conversion, he became an involved member of a church, including teaching Sunday School.

Some people come to Jesus because they are afraid of what would happen to them after they die. The hymn, "Tell It To Jesus" (Rankin/Lorence) asks "Are you troubled at the thought of dying?"

It urges people to "Tell it to Jesus" since "He is a friend that's well known."

EXTERNAL FACTORS

Miracles. Many theologians rightly maintain that conversion, itself, is a miracle because how else could someone who is steeped in sin do a "180" and begin living a Christians life style? The apostle Paul is perhaps the best example of such a complete turnaround. One day he is on the road to Damascus to capture Christians and return them to Jerusalem for punishment—a manifestation of his persecution of them and his denial of Christ—and a short time later he is preaching "Christ in the synagogues, that He is the Son of God" (Acts 9:20).

There are a number of scriptures that provide examples of miracles (or "signs," "works," or "wonders"). Jesus in John 10:37-38 makes a general statement about the power of miracles to bring about salvation: scriptures that provide examples of miracles (or "signs," "works," or "wonders") leading to salvation. "If I do not the works of my Father believe me not. But if I do, though ye believe me not, believe the works: that ye may know and believe that the Father is in me, and I in him").

1. When Jesus spoke to the one cleansed heper who thanked Him for being healed He said: "Arise, go thy way: thy faith made thee whole" (Luke 17:19). (The note on this passage says that it may be rendered "thy faith hath saved thee").

2. Jesus responded this way to the blind man who received his sight and thanked Him: "...thy faith saved thee" (Luke 18:42).

3. "Now when he was in Jerusalem at the Passover in the feast day many believed in his name when they saw the miracles which He did' (John 2:23).

4. After the nobleman realized that Jesus had saved his son from death, "he himself believed and his whole house" (John 4:53).

5. When Jesus taught in the Temple, "many believed on Him, and said, when Christ cometh, will He do more miracles than these which this man hath done?" (John 7:31).
6. After Jesus raised Lazarus from the dead, many Jews believed on Him (John 12: 9-11).
7. When Jesus predicted his resurrection, He said: "And now I have told you before it come to pass, that, when it is come to pass, ye might believe"
8. When the apostle John entered the tomb where Jesus had been buried and saw that it was empty, he believed (John 20:8).
9. Jesus' brothers only believed that he was the Messiah after his resurrection (John 7:5 and Acts 1:14).
10. The apostle Thomas believed that Jesus was the Messiah only after he thrust his finger into the side of Jesus' resurrected body (John 20: 24-29).
11. "And many other signs truly did Jesus in the presence of his disciples, which are not written in this book: But these are written, that ye might believe that Jesus is the Christ, the Son of God, and that believing ye might have life through His name" (John 20: 30-31).
12. When Peter raised Tabitha (Dorcas) from the dead, many believed in the Lord (Acts 9:36).

Many theologians maintain that there have been no miracles since the apostolic age. The author, respectfully, disagrees. Millions of people have been saved since then; it was indicated earlier that salvation, itself, is a miracle. And there are many miracles that people have cited to explain their conversion. These include being cured of "incurable" cancer, escaping unscathed from an horrific traffic accident, having a "small voice" tell someone to go to a certain location at a specific time whereupon a complete stranger will witness to them (Phillip was told by the Holy Spirit to go to a certain location in Gaza so he could witness to an Ethiopian eunuch), a person deciding at the last minute to not board a plane which crashes, the birth of a child to a couple who were told that they could never have children, someone being pronounced dead and then returing to life 30 minutes later, flowers blooming every Spring, trees regrowing leaves on an annual basis, an alcoholic or drug addict suddenly becoming sober and remaining sober, receipt of unexpected money when a bank account is about to have insufficient funds, and so on.

Whittaker Chambers was a Communist who spied for the Soviet Union mainly in the 1930s. He had a change of heart, renounced Communism, and stopped spying. He tried to get his best friend, Alger Hiss, to also stop spying for the Russians but to no avail.

Chambers warned our government about the danger of Communism but nothing was done. At the beginning of the 1950s, as a senior editor with Time, he was involved in a sensational trial in which he accused Hiss of being a Soviet spy. He was despondent to have to confront his former friend, had feared for his life after renouncing Communism, and was being reviled in the press.

Chambers eventually got peace of mind after committing himself to the Lord and becoming a member of the Quaker faith. What prompted him to turn his life around? One day he was holding his infant daughter and looked closely at her ear and decided that this was a miracle that could only have been created by God.

Family Members. Some people become born again because someone in their family is born again and successfully witnesses to them. Two examples are found in the Bible. When the Philippian jailer asked his prisoners, Paul and Silas, what he needed to do to be saved, the responses were "Believe on the Lord Jesus Christ, and thou shalt be saved, AND THY HOUSE (emphasis added; Acts 16:27-31). When a nobleman realized that Jesus had healed his son "who was at the point of death," he "himself believed, and his WHOLE HOUSE" (John 4:53), emphasis added).

I believe that similarly, today, one saved person in a household often serves as the catalyst for everyone else in that household becoming born again.

People Outside The Family Sometimes, people who are outside a household can bring acquaintances to salvation. Friends in high school or college or Sunday School classes, colleagues at work, members of athletic teams or workout groups, people met randomly in super markets or on the street, etc. can be instrumental in bringing someone to the Lord.

<u>Scriptures.</u> Some people become saved by reading the scriptures. Some of the passages that have already been cited in this book may be helpful or others may be the stimulus needed, especially those about Jesus and his sacrificial death on the cross.

<u>Television and Radio Broadcasters.</u> There are a number of individual programs and Christian networks that carry Christian programming and music. The networks that come readily to mind are CBN (Christian Broadcasting Network) and TBN (Trinity Broadcasting Network). There are some that are totally online, as well. Some are national, even international in scope, while others may have a regional or local audience.

I personally like to listen to KHCB (Keeping Him Close By) a radio station out of Houston with a regional outreach. Specific programs that I find enriching are Alastair Begg, David Jeremiah, Nancy Lee DeMoss, Adrian Rogers, J. Vernon McGhee, and Donald Grey Barnhouse.

Unless a specific program emphasizes salvation through Jesus Christ, including an invitation to accept Him as Lord and Savior—and righteous Christian living, I would be very reluctant to tune in. Be especially wary of broadcasts that emphasize a "prosperity gospel," that is, you will be blessed with income and wealth if you accept Jesus as Lord and savior—and send a generous contribution to the program.

<u>Literature.</u> Books, pamphlets, and tracts that emphasize the need to accept God's grace through Jesus Christ, His Son, in order to receive salvation, are often the impetus by which people are saved.

<u>Local Churches and Pastors.</u> The major responsibility of local churches and their pastors is to preach the need for sinners to receive Christ as their Lord and Savior. If you are seeking salvation or are already saved and want to live a righteous life, do not attend churches that do not have these orientations. If you are already in such a church, get out as quickly as you can. My mother—more about her later in this chapter—used to squirm in her pew seat as one of the pastors continually quoted irrelevant poetry, for example,

"flower in the crannied wall." She would come home after church, distraught, asking "why couldn't he just tell us about Jesus?"

Pastors need to issue an "altar call" at the end of their services which encourages people to come forth to ask Jesus' forgiveness for their sins. Many people have been saved by "going forward," such as, the millions who have done so at the various Billy Graham crusades.

Bringing people to a personal relationship with Jesus should never be subservient to extracurricular activities that seem to predominate in many churches. Year ago, I heard a young, female speaker at a church my wife and I were attending who admonished churches that over-emphasized such activities as "jogging for Jesus" and "karate for Christ."

<u>Martyrs.</u> Some men and women have been led to accept Christ as their Lord and savior because they were in awe of the sacrifices made by Christian martyrs.

As recorded in the Bible, the first Christian martyr was Stephen (Acts 6 and 7). Stephen is referred to as "a man full of faith and of the Holy Ghost" (Acts 6:5). Acts 6:8 states that he "did great wonders and miracles among the people." Because of his witnessing about Christ, he offended some Jews in various synagogues which resulted in his being brought before the Jewish Council and the high priest. (When they looked on him, they "saw his face as it had been the face of an "angel"—Acts 6:15). Stephen's response to the high priest's question, "Are these things so?" (Acts 7:1) so incensed the Jewish rulers "they were cut to the heart, and they gnashed on him with their teeth," (Acts 7:54) and "they cried out with a loud voice, and stopped their ears, and ran upon him with one accord" (Acts 7:57) that resulted in him being stoned. (See Acts 7:2-53 for Stephen's entire discourse).

As Stephen died, he said: "Lord, lay not this sin to their charge" (Acts 7:60). Note how similar this utterance is to Christ's words on the cross: "Father, forgive them; for they know not what they do" (Luke 23:34).

The 11 apostles of Jesus—Judas is excluded because he hung himself as is John because he died a natural death in old age; Matthias replaced Judas—all were martyred because of their preaching salvation through Jesus Christ:

Peter—crucified upside down.
Andrew—burned to death
James, the son of Zebedee--beheaded by Herod
Philip—crucified upside down
Bartholomew—crucified upside down
Thomas—pierced with spears
Matthew—burned alive
James, the son of Alphaeus—stoned and clubbed
Thaddeus—beaten to death with clubs
Simon the Canaanite (or "Zealot")—crucified
Matthias—burned to death

There have been millions of Christian martyrs since the deaths of these 11 apostles, many at the hands of Moslems whose faith is Islam. Turkey, a Moslem nation, exterminated around two million Armenian Christians during and immediately after World War 1. During the 1990s, Sudan murdered more than one million Black Christians who lived in the south because they did not want to remain part of that Islamic nation. More than 200,000 Catholics living in East Timor were slaughtered by the government of Indonesia, a Moslem nation, in the 1990s. And, recently, we have become aware of atrocities committed by ISIS and other Islamic groups, especially in Syria, Iraq, and North Africa. The one act which particularly upset me was the beheadings of the Coptic Christians in Libya—all fine looking young men who were only trying to find work to support their families.

2 Corinthians 11:23-28 delineates the various hardships Paul had to endure as a missionary for the Lord. These include stripes, being imprisoned, beaten, stoned, ship-wrecked, hunger and thirst, weariness, pain, cold, nakedness, weakness, and being offended.

GOD'S INITIATIVE

Sometimes, God will approach an unsaved person in such a dramatic way that he or she will become saved, even if, at that time, they had no intention or even a desire to be saved, or did not even know what salvation was. Two examples come to mind.

Consider what happened to Saul (later called Paul). Our discussion of him earlier in this chapter clearly indicated that while on the road to Damascus, he was certainly not doing so because he desired to be born again and wanted to visit his Christian brothers and sisters in Damascus. But because of contact initiated by God—a light from Heaven and Jesus talking to him and asking Saul why he was persecuting Him, striking him blind, and telling him to continue his journey to Damascus--Saul became born again and began a ministry of witnessing to Gentiles.

My mother's experience is another example of God intervening in someone's life that resulted in their conversion. In the spring of 1955, we three boys were sitting in the living room when she walked in from outside, Dad behind her, and he announced that he was leaving her for another woman (18 years mom's junior) and that they were getting a divorce. As he was leaving, she asked "what about the twins (I and my brother; we were 17 at the time) and their going to college?" His response was essentially that he could care less.

I realized some years later that this circumstance caused her to go into a deep depression, triggered by a feeling of rejection: her mother had rejected her as a child. Although she continued to marginally function, she told me later that she considered going to our barn, throwing a rope over one of its beams, and hanging herself.

One day, she was sitting under our black walnut tree. Sudently, she realized that Jesus Christ was standing next to her. He told her: "Don't worry Lenor. Everything will be all right."

After this encounter, she turned the corner. She was able to deal with her husband's rejection and forgave him for what he had one. She began witnessing to people, including the three sons. She read the Bible consistently, listened to and watched radio and television programs featuring Christian pastors and evangelists, attended church regularly, and taught the Junior High Sunday school class for 25 years.

I can assure the reader that when she sat under that black walnut trees, she was not asking to be saved but, rather, was crying out in agony and despair when God intervened through Jesus Christ, His Son.

IS THERE AN APPROPRIATE TIME TO BE SAVED?

Many people feel called to commit themselves to the Lord, to be saved, but for some reason, do not respond. They feel that they might be looked upon as needing a crutch that won't resonate positively with their circle of friends, they want to think about it, they will do it tomorrow, why today when the opportunity will always be there?

There is danger in waiting. You may never again be drawn to commit yourself to Jesus, your friends may talk you out of it, some tragedy may cause you to become angry with God and turn you away from His invitation, and you may be killed that very evening in a car accident.

The Bible is adamant about not delaying an invitation to accept God's offer of salvation. 2 Corinthians 6:2 states: "For He saith, I have heard thee in a time accepted, and in the day of salvation have I have succored thee: behold, now is the day of salvation. The hymn, "Why Not Now?.," (Nath/Case) says "You have wandered far away; Do not risk another day; Do not turn from God your face; But today accept his grace. "Softly And Tenderly" (Thompson) contains these lyrics: "Why should we tarry when Jesus is pleading, Pleading 'for you and for me?"

HYMNS

Here are some great, well-known hymns that speak gloriously of salvation:

"And my sins which were many are all washed away" ("Since Jesus Came Into My Heart," McDaniel/Gabriel).

"Oh, the love that drew salvation's plan, Oh, the grace that bro't it down to man". (At Calvary," Newell/Towner).

"Hail him who saved you by His grace" ("All Hail The Power," Perronet/Ellor).

"Amazing grace! How sweet the sound that saved a wretch like me" ("Amazing Grace," Newton/Excell).

"And sinners plunged beneath the flood, Lose all their guilty stains" ("There Is A Foundation Filled With Blood," Cowper/Mason).

CHAPTER THREE

THE COMPONENTS OF SALVATION: GOD'S ROLE

> "Neither is there salvation in any other: for there is none other name under heaven given among men, whereby we must be saved" (Acts 4:12).

IN THIS CHAPTER, WE WILL BEGAN TO TAKE a close and comprehensive look at the phenomenon of salvation. In this chapter, we are concerned with salvation from God's perspective. In Chapter Four, we will focus on salvation from man's perspective.

We will need to examine salvation in these contexts for several reasons. First, we as Christians should be interested in gaining a deeper understanding of the most momentous occurrence in our lives. Second, we will come to appreciate the fact that salvation is multi-dimensional, that is, there are multiple components of what God does with us through His grace. Third, as we become aware of these aspects of salvation, we will arrive at a deeper appreciation of what God's love has done for us. Fourth, as we meditate on these elements of salvation, we can become more specific when we thank our Heavenly Father for saving us by identifying those aspects of salvation that we believe are particularly relevant for us. Fifth, because many of these components of salvation are often confusing for even mature Christians, the following discussion will, hopefully, result in a clearer understanding as to what they mean. Sixth, as we witness to non-believers, we may be better able to refer to those specific aspects of salvation that will be of most concern to them, thus increasing the likelihood that they will become born again.

Exhibit 3.1 shows that grace, God's love for us, is the wellspring (the inner circle) from which the 13 components of salvation (contained in the second circle) are derived.

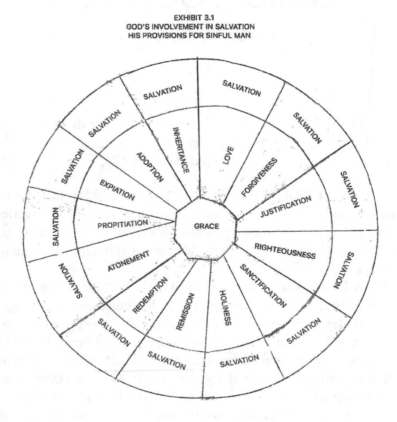

EXHIBIT 3.1
GOD'S INVOLVEMENT IN SALVATION
HIS PROVISIONS FOR SINFUL MAN

As indicated earlier, there is another side to salvation: man's side. Frankly, I was not early-on convinced that it was appropriate to portray salvation from this two-sided perspective until I was studying the book of Psalms. In discussing salvation—usually through the prayers of King David—references occur to both "MY salvation" (David's perspective) and "THY salvation" (God's perspective). In all, there were 22 references in this book to "my salvation" and six to "our salvation" and 24 to "thy salvation" plus two each to "salvation of the Lord or God" and eight to "His salvation."

Here are some of the psalms that refer to "my salvation:"

Psalm 25:5—"Lead me in thy truth, and teach me, For thou art that God of my salvation."

Psalm 18:46:--"The Lord liveth; and blessed be my rock. And let the God of my salvation be exalted."

Psalm 27:1—"The Lord is my light and my salvation. Whom shall I fear?"

Psalm 88:11—"O Lord God of my salvation. I have cried day and night before thee."

Psalm 118:14—"The Lord is my strength and song. And is become my salvation."

Below are some of the psalms that refer to "thy salvation:"

Psalm 9:14—"That I may shew forth all thy praise in the gates of the daughters of Zion. I will rejoice in thy salvation."

Psalm 13:5—"But I have trusted in thy mercy. My heart shall rejoice in thy salvation."

Psalm 85:7—Shew us thy mercy, O Lord, and grant us thy salvation."

Psalm 106:4—"Remember me, O Lord, with the favour that Thou bearest unto the people. O visit me with thy salvation."

Psalm 119:81—"My soul fainteth for thy salvation. But I hope in thy word."

Before the specific aspects of salvation are discussed, it is appropriate for the reader to be aware of the process that the author employed to get a better grasp on the meaning and significance of the various components of salvation. The first activity involved my reading the New Testament twice. While doing this, I recorded every passage and its location that mentioned any of these aspects of salvation. I was especially interested in the context of each, with particular emphasis on who was involved, did anyone specifically ask what was required to be saved, to whom was the question directed (Jesus, obviously, being of paramount importance), and what was the response to that question (Jesus' being the most significant). The total number of times each salvation element was contained in the New Testament was determined and was corroborated by using Strong's Exhaustive Concordance. It can be argued that the number of times each salvation concept is mentioned in the NT is indicative of its importance. Thus, as each of the 13 aspects of salvation are discussed, the number of times it occurs in the New Testament will be indicated.

As informative as the King James Study Bible and its accompanying notes are, the author also felt compelled to use the various reference sources contained at the end of this book in order to obtain more incisive and complete understanding of these salvation components. However, in some cases, the definitions offered by these reference sources were not as instructive as I hoped, so I consulted various dictionaries and other sources found on the Internet.

As this process evolved, I noticed that, in some instances, different terminology was used to represent the same salvation aspect. Nevertheless, because these differing definitions are often employed by respected Biblical scholars and may contribute at least marginally to a better understanding of the concepts, occasionally several definitions are offered as the salvation components are discussed.

In some instances, Biblical scholars consider some salvation constructs to be a subset of a more comprehensive one. Because the author believed that these subsidiary concepts may enhance reader understanding of the overarching concept, I decided to include both the umbrella concept and the subsidiary ones in the discussion.

So as to enrich the reader's understanding of the ideas presented in Chapters Three, I have included excerpts from hymns that most appropriately deal with each of the aspects of salvation that are discussed in this chapter.

SALVATION

The word, "salvation," appears 45 times in the New Testament. Interestingly, Jesus used it only twice. In Luke 19:9, our Lord said when He had the encounter with Zacchaeus: "This day is salvation come to this house, forasmuch as he also is a son of Abraham." He said in John 4:22, when talking to the samaritan woman at the well: "Ye worship ye know not what: for salvation is of the Jews."

Other passages in the NT that I believe best capture the notion of salvation include the following:

> Acts: 4:2—"Neither is there salvation in any other: for there is none other name under Heaven given among men, whereby we must be saved."

> Acts 13:47—"For so hath the Lord commanded us, saying, I have set thee to be a light of the Gentiles that thou shouldest be for salvation unto the ends of the earth." (Paul and Barnabas speaking about why they were witnessing to non-Jews).

> Acts 16:17—"The same followed Paul and us, and cried, saying, These men are the servants of the most high God, which shew unto us the way

of salvation." (Comment of a "certain damsel possessed with a spirit of divination").

Acts 28:28—"Be it known therefore unto you, that
the salvation of God is unto the Gentiles, and that
they will hear it."

Romans 1:16—"For I am not ashamed of the gospel
of Christ: for it is the power of God unto salvation
to everyone who believeth, to the Jew first, and also
to the Greek."

2 Corinthians 6:2—"....behold, now is the accepted
time; behold, now is the day of salvation."

2 Timothy 2:10—"Therefore, I endure all things for
the elects' sakes, that they may also obtain the salvation which is in Christ Jesus with eternal glory."

Titus 2:11—"For the grace of God that brigneth salvation hath appeared to all men."

Revelation 12:10 –"And I heard a loud voice saying
in Heaven, now is come salvation, and strength, and
the kingdom of our God" (the apostle John's words
after Satan's banishment from Heaven).

Jesus uttered the word, "saved," 10 times in the NT. The most
significant of these include Matthew 10:22 ("...but he that endureth
to the end shall be saved"), Luke 7:50 ("and he said to her, woman,
thy faith hath saved thee...") and John 3:17 ("For God sent not
his Son into the world to condemn the world; but that the world
through Him might be saved").

We can draw several conclusions concerning the notion of salvation based on the above passages. The only path to salvation is
through Jesus. Salvation is available to both Jews and Gentiles.
Belief appears to be a pre-condition for salvation (more about belief

in Chapter Four). If an unsaved person feels drawn to Jesus by the Holy Spirit, that man or woman should accept Him right away and not put that decision off. It is important for the saved person to be steadfast in his or her Christian walk throughout their lives—more about this obligation in Chapter Six.

GRACE

It can be argued that grace is the over arching manifestation of God's love for mankind, from which all of the components of salvation are derived. (This is why, in Exhibit 3.1, the "grace circle" is placed at the center of this diagram),

Grace is usually defined as an unmerited gift from a superior (God) to an inferior (mankind). One reference is more instructive when it defines grace as the "undeserved favor of God in providing salvation for those deserving condemnation" (Brand, Draper and England) because we have all sinned. (In the Old Testament, the word "favor" is often used to represent "grace").

Ephesians 1:4 ("According as he hath chosen us in Him before the foundation of the world, that we should be holy and without blame before him in love") and 2 Timothy 1:9 ("Who hath saved us, and called us with a holy calling, not according to our works, but according to His own purpose and grace, which was given us in Christ Jesus before the world began") indicate, according to one source (Smith), that the gift of grace by God was in His divine plan from the very beginning.

Grace and works are never commingled; that is, works can never result in the granting of grace. The most relevant Bible scripture that supports this principle is, of course, Ephesians 2: 8-9: "For by grace are ye saved through faith; and that not of yourselves: it is the gift of God: not of works, lest any man should boast."

While the word, "grace," appear in the New Testament about 120 times, 2 Corinthians 12:9 is the only one in which Jesus uses the word grace. The apostle, Paul, prayed three times that God would remove a serious affliction ("a thorn in the flesh"). The response, in denying this request, was "My grace is sufficient for thee: for my strength is made perfect in weakness."

The importance of God's grace in the New Testament is evidenced by the fact that this concept is frequently used in the salutations contained in the very beginning of various New Testament books, usually the epistles. For example, 2 Corinthians 1:2, says: "Grace be to you and peace from God our Father, and from the Lord Jesus Christ." The same salutation is also found in Galatians, Philippians, Colossians, and 1 Timothy (also Paul's epistles),

Grace is often employed in Paul's epistles as a benediction. In Romans 16:24, he writes: "The grace of our lord Jesus Christ be with you all. Amen." He uses the exact same verbiage to conclude 2 Thessalonians. The apostle, Peter, ends 2 Peter with "But grow in grace..." Perhaps, significantly, the concluding verse in the entire Bible, Revelation 21:22 reads "The grace of our Lord Jesus Christ be with you all. Amen."

There are many hymns, a number of which are well-known to Christians, that address the notion of grace. Some of these are:

> "Amazing Grace" (Newton/Excell): "Amazing grace! How sweet the sound that saved a wretch like me."

> "Saved" (Smith/Hickman): "Saved! Saved! Saved! By grace and grace alone."

> "Glorious Things Of Thee Are Spoken" (Newton/Haydn): "Grace which, like the Lord, The Giver, Never fails from age to age."

> O That Will Be Glory" (Gabriel/Gabriel): "When, by the gift of His infite grace, I am accorded in Heaven a place."

> "At Calvary" (Newell/Towner): "Mercy there was great, and grace was free."

> "O That Will be Glory" (Gabriel/Gabriel): "When by His grace, I shall look on His Face."

"Wonderful Grace Of Jesus" (Lillenas/Lillenas):
"Wonderful grace of Jesus, Greater than all my sin."

LOVE

1 John 4:8 succinctly states: "God is love." The accompanying note in the KJV Study Bible indicates that He manifests love in His essential nature and in all of His actions. Love is God's dominant quality. Youngblood maintains that the greatest example of God's love is that He sent His Son to die on the cross for our sins. His love for believers is everlasting and never fails or is diminished.

The Bible addresses three types of love: eros, phileo, and agape. Eros refers to the erotic love between the sexes. Phileo represents tender affection, usually directed to a friend or family member. It also epitomizes God's love for His Son, Jesus (see John 5:20). Agape love is used by believers to denote God's unconditional love for them (Brand, Draper and English).

There are many well-known hymns that portray God's love. Some of these are:

"Jesus Loves Me" (Bradbury): "Jesus loves me! This I know for the Bible tells me so."

"Love Lifted Me" (Rowe/Smith): "Love lifted me.... Love lifted me!...When nothing else could help, Love lifted me."

"Such Love" (Bishop/Markness): "That God should love a sinner such as I, How wonderful is love like this."

"Tell Me The Old, Old Story" (Hankey/Doane): "Tell me the old, old story of Jesus and His love."

FORGIVENESS

Forgiveness is probably the God-instituted aspect of salvation that Christians and non-believers are most familiar with. Indeed, for those men and women who become saved, the expectation of forgiveness may have been the driving force behind their conversion: they plead guilty to their sin-filled life, and asked for forgiveness. Therefore, it is appropriate that it should be the first of the God-given elements of salvation to be discussed.

The Aid To Bible Understanding defines forgiveness as "The art of pardoning an offender: ceases to feel resentment toward him because of his offense and giving up all claims to recompense." Brand, Draper and England reveal that the words, "trespasses" and "debts" are some times used synonymously for sins in some Biblical passages. Example: In the Lord's Prayer (Matthew 6:12), Jesus talks about sinners petitioning God for forgiveness of their "debts."

Some Biblical passages referring to forgiveness do not deal with the forgivnesses by God of man's sins. They, instead, refer to the need for people to forgive other people who have hurt or wronged them. (The Lord's Prayer instructs us to "forgive us our debtors").

The reader will note that the subsequent discussions of God's involvement with salvation appear to overlap to some extent with forgiveness. This is perhaps understandable given that the apostle, Paul, tended to use "righteousness" and "redemption" as surrogates for "forgiveness."

Following are some of the Biblical passages that deal with forgiveness, with special emphasis on those that contain the words of Jesus (There are 52 references to "Forgive," "Forgiven' or "Forgiveness" in the NT; 39 are spoken by Jesus):

1. Matthew 9:5—"For whether is easier to say Thy sins be forgiven thee..." (Jesus talking to the Jewish scribes when he healed a man with palsy).
2. Luke 7:48—Jesus talking to the woman who anointed His feet: "Thy sins are forgiven."

3. Colossians 2:13: "...having forgiven you all trespasses." (The apostle Paul's letter to the Colossians designed to refute heretical teaching).
4. 1 John 2:12—"I write unto you little children because your sins are forgiven.
5. Ephesians 1:7—"In whom we have redemption through His blood, the forgiveness of sins, according to the riches of His grace."
6. Mark 11:25—Jesus on prayer: "And when ye stand praying, forgive if ye have ought against any: That your Father also which is in heaven may forgive your trespasses."
7. Luke 17:3 – "Take heed to yourselves: if thy brother trespass against thee, rebuke him; and if he repent; thou shalt forgive him."
8. Matthew 9:2—Jesus talking to the palsied man he healed: "Son, be of good cheer; thy sins be forgiven."

There are two hymns that offer lyrics pertaining to forgiveness. These include "I Will Praise Him" (Harris): "Glory, glory to the Son....He's forgiven my transgressions" and "Let Him In" (Atchinson/Excell): "He will speak your sins forgiven...He will take you to heaven!"

There is a popular song that debuted in 1954 and became a huge hit. It was composed by J. Richards, R. Mullan, and B. Feldman and was sung by Al Hibler and the McGuire sisters. Some of the lyrics of "He" are." Though it makes him sad to see the way we live, He'll always say 'I forgive."

JUSTIFICATION

Justification has been defined as the "absolving or clearing of any charge, or to hold as guiltless, to acquit, or to pronounce and treat as righteous." Justification occurs through God's grace. The cases for justification are the works of Jesus, His death on the cross and His resurrection. The justified person can look forward to peace with God, access to Him, the resurrection of his body, and an eternal inheritance. The justified person is expected to do good works after his conversion. (Aid To Bible Understanding)

There are 35 verses in the New Testament that deal with justification; six are attributed to Jesus. The most relevant are:

> Matthew 12:37—"For by words thou shalt be justified…" (Jesus' words).

> Romans 3:24—"Being justified freely by his grace, through the redemption that is in Jesus Christ."

> Romans 4:25—"Who was delivered for our offenses and was raised again for our justification." (Reference is, of course, to Jesus).

> Romans 5:1—"Therefore being justified by faith, we have peace with our God through our Lord, Jesus Christ."

> Romans 5:9—"Much more then being now justified by his blood, we shall be saved from wrath through Him."

> Romans 5:18—"Therefore as by the offense of one, judgement came upon all men to condemnation; even so by the righteousness of one, the free gift came upon all men unto justification of life."

> Galatians 3:8—"And the scripture, foreseeing that God would justify the heathen through faith, preached before the gospel unto Abraham, saying, In thee shall all nations be blessed."

> Titus 3:7—"That being justified by His grace, we should be made heirs according to the hope of eternal life."

There is a famous hymn, "One Day" (Chapman/Marsh) that deals with the topic of justification. The relevant lyrics are "Living, He loved me; dying He saved me; Buried, He carried my sins far away; Rising, He justified freely forever: One day He's coming— Oh, glorious day!"

RIGHTEOUSNESS

Since the fall of man in the Garden of Eden, man has essentially been viewed by God as unrighteous. Righteousness, on the other hand, is viewed as holy and upright living.

Man cannot obtain righteousness through his own efforts. God views a person as being righteous when he or she has accepted Jesus Christ as their Lord and savior. In effect, God transfers (imputes) His own righteousness to those believers who have trusted in His Son (Romans 4:15, Galatians 3:6 and Philippians 3:9). God sees us as being righteous because of our identification by faith with His Son.

The degree to which righteousness exists in a believer is represented by the extent to which that person conforms to the will of God. In the Old Testament book of Proverbs, a righteous person is viewed as being honest, generous, steadfast, courageous, merciful, and just (Brand, Draper and England). In the Bible, there are many people who are designated as being "righteous." Perhaps the best known are Noah, Abraham, Job, David, Enoch, Abel, Moses, John the Baptist, Paul, and Joseph (Mary's husband), as well as, of course, Jesus Christ.

There are 101 references in the Bible to "righteousness" and 41 to "righteous," The first set of verses below are those that contain the words of Jesus and confirm that believers are considered by God to be righteous.

Matthew 13:43—"Then shall the righteous shine forth as the sun in the kingdom of their Father."

Matthew 23:35—"That upon you may come all the righteous blood shed upon the Earth, from the blood of righteous Abel…"

Matthew 25:37—"Then shall the righteous answer Him, saying, Lord when we saw thee a hungred, and fed thee, or thirsty and gave thee drink." (Jesus talking about the final judgment based on who helped the Jews during the "Great Tribulation").

Matthew 25:46—"And these shall go away into everlasting punishment: but the righteous into life eternal."

There are many more indications in the New Testament—in the words of the apostles—that believers will be accorded righteousness:

Luke 1:74—"That He would grant unto us, that we being delivered out of the hands of our enemies, might serve Him without fear, In holiness and righteousness, before Him, all the days of our lives."

Romans 5:17—"For if by one man's offence death reigned by one; much more they which receive abundance of grace and the gift of righteousness shall reign in life by one, Jesus Christ."

Romans 5:21—"That as sin hath reigned unto death, even so might grace reign through righteousness unto eternal life by Jesus Christ our Lord,"

Romans 6:18—"Being made free from sin, ye became the servant s of righteousness."

1 Peter 2:24—""Who his own self bare our sins in his own body on the tree, that we, being dead to sins,

should live unto righteousness by whose stripes we were healed."

Romans 5:19—"For as one man's disobedience, many were made sinners, so by the obedience of one should many be made righteous."

1 Peter 3:12—"For the eyes of the Lord are over the righteous and his ears are open unto their prayers."

One of the most revered hymns, "The Solid Rock" (Mote/Bradbury), contains these lyrics: "My hope is built on nothing less than Jesus' blood and righteousness...On Christ the solid rock I stand, All other ground is sinking sand." "Called Unto Holiness" (Morris/Morris) states: "Not on our righteousness, but Christ within, Living and reigning and saving from sin." The words, "God's eyes are on the righteous; his ears hear their cry, He knows when they got trouble, He will answer by and by," are contained in the song, "God's Eyes Are On The Righteous" (The Paynes).

SANCTIFICATION

The concept of sanctification is aptly captured in three definitions taken from three reference sources. Youngblood defines it as the "process of God's grace by which the believer is separated from sin and becomes dedicated to God's righteousness." The Aid To Bible Understanding views sanctification as the "act or process of making holy or of separation apart for the service or use of Jehovah God." Brand, Draper and England define it as the "process of being holy resulting in a changed life style for the believer."

There are some similarities in these definitions. First, there is the notion of separation. Second, there is the idea that justification is a process. Third, there is an expectation that, as part of this process, the believer will render some type of service to God.

In regard to the second and third points, the Aid To Bible Understanding says: "Christians must maintain their sanctification to the end of their earthly course." 2 Timothy 2:21-22 elaborates on this mandate by stating that the sanctified person must "follow righteousness, faith, charity, peace, with them that call on the Lord out of a pure heart."

The term, "sanctified," occurs 16 times in the New Testament. In three instances, Jesus' words are observed. "Sanctification" occurs five times. Jesus does not use this word at all. "Sanctifieth" occurs four times; twice it is used by our Lord. "Sanctify" appears six times; Jesus uttered it twice.

In John 10:36, Jesus said: "Say ye of Him, whom the Father hath sanctified, and sent into the world, Thou blasphemest; because I said, I am the Son of God?" In John 7:19, Jesus' words are found: "that they might be sanctified through the truth." This is a reference to God consecrating us to service according to the accompanying note. Our Lord used the words, "sanctified by faith" (Acts 26:18) to signify "set apart for the Lord". (See note on 1 Corinthians 1:2). In confronting the Pharisees (Matthew 23:17), He said "ye fools and blind; for whether is greater, the gold, or the temple that sanctifieth the gold?" He uses a similar analogy in Matthew 33:19, involving the gift or the altar that sanctifieth the gift.

There are numerous references to sanctification in the Old Testament. As might be expected, many of theses involve people — priests, Levites, Nazarites (Sampson for one), Moses, Noah, and so on — but also:

Places: Jerusalem, the Garden of Eden, Mount Sinai, cities of refuge.

Things: The temple, ark of the covenant, altar of incense, table of shew bread, lampstand, altar of burnt offerings, basin, utensils, incense, anointing oil, priestly garments, sacifices, food, and tithes.

Times or Occasions: Seventh day (creation and the Sabbath), feast days, year of jubilee.

Land: Part of inheritance for God to be set aside for Him, west-east strips of land granted to each of Israel's twelve tribes (see Aid To Bible Understanding).

Our Lord addresses His apostles in John 17:17 this way: "Sanctify them through thy truth: thy word is truth." (The note on this verse defines "sanctify" as "to set apart for sacred use" or to make holy". Jesus' prouncement in John 17:19 that "for their sakes (the apostles), I sanctify myself" is interpreted in the note to mean that Jesus is setting Himself apart to do God's will.

There is one hymn that I found that deals with sanctification. This is the "Old Rugged Cross" (Bennard/Bennard); the relevant lyrics are: "For 'twas on that old rugged cross Jesus suffered and died To pardon and sanctify me."

HOLINESS

The paramount characteristic of "holiness" is that believers are set apart, that is, we are set apart from unrighteousness and are set apart for God. This second aspect suggests that there are obligations to God that we are expected to fulfill as believers.

These two elements are found in two statements in leading references. "We were set apart to God, that in conversion, and we are living out that dedication to God in holiness" (Brand, Draper and England). "Sanctification, or true holiness, is expressed in patient and loving service to God while awaiting the Lord's return" (Youngblood).

An interesting aspect of hoiness was made by Rene Malgo, Midnight Call (April, 2016) who maintains that living a holy life ("separation from sin, immorality and decency") "give us confidence in our salvation" (Romans 6:22).

The Bible expands the notion of holiness beyond believers. Of course, God, Jesus and the Holy Spirit are considered holy, as are places (holy ground, the tabernacle, military camps), periods of time (Passover, Pentecost or Festival of Booths, Sabbath, Sabbath year, year of jubilee), objects (ark of the covenant, altar of sacrifice, anointing oil, priestly garments, furniture in the sanctuary), animals and produce (first-born cattle, sheep and goats and first fruits), and tithes (Aid To Bible Understanding).

There are numerous passages in the New Testament—175 references involving "holy" and 13 that allude to "holiness"—that confirm that believers are considered by God to be holy. (Jesus uses the word "Holy" 16 tmes, but did not utter "holiness" one time). Some of these are:

Ephesians 1:4—"According as He hath chosen us in Him before the foundation of the world, that we should be holy and without blame before Him in love." (The note on this passage states that "Holiness is the result—not the basis of God's choosing").

Colossians 1:22—"In the body of His flesh through death, to preserve you holy and unblameable and unreproveable in His sight."

1 Thessalonians 5:27—"I charge you by the Lord that this epistle be read unto all the holy brethren."

1 Peter 1:15—"But as He which called you is holy, so be ye holy in all manner of conversation."

1 Peter 1:16—"Because it is written, Be ye holy, for I am holy."

2 Peter 1:21—"For the prophecy came not in old times by the will of man: but holy men of God spake as they were moved by the Holy Ghost."

Ephesians 4:24—"And that ye put on the new man which after God is created in righteousness and true holiness."

1 Thessalonians 3:13—"To the end he may stablish your hearts unblameable in holiness before God."

Hebrews 12:10—"For they verily for a few days chastended us after their own pleasure; but He for our profit, that we might be partakers of His holiness."

There are several hymns that refer to "holiness" or "holy." "Take Time To Be Holy" (Longstaff/Stebbins) has these lyrics: "Take time to be holy, Speak oft with the Lord…" "Make friends of God's children." The hymn, "Holy in Me" (Bible/Nettleton) informs us: "Not by training to be holy, But in you the holy one." "You are more than I could hope for. You're holy now in me" are words found in "Greater Than My Words" (Bible/Bible). The hymn, "Called Unto To Holiness" (Morris/Morris), states: "Called unto Holiness, praise His dear name." The hymn, "More Holiness Give Me" (Bliss), asks God: "More holiness give me, more striving within."

REMISSION

Remission is frequently used in conjunction with sin. As such, remission is essentially employed as a synonym for "forgiveness." Thus, "remission of sins" signifies release from the guilt or penalty associated with sin.

Remission is available due to Jesus' sacrificial death on the cross. It is available to all who believe in the name of Jesus (Acts 10:43, see below). Often, in the New Testament, remission appears with "repentance" (see Chapter Four for discussion of repentance).

Below are some Biblical references that deal with remission ("Remission" appears 10 times in the N.T. and include two utterances by Jesus)".

> Matthew 26:28—"For this is my blood of the New
> Testament, which is shed for the remission of sins"
> (Jesus' statement about himself).

> Luke 3:3—"And he (John the Baptist) came into all
> the country about Jordan, preaching the baptism of
> repentance for the remission of sins."

> Luke 24:47—" And that repentance and remission
> of sins should be preached in His name among all
> nations, beginning at Jerusalem." (Jesus' words
> directed to the apostles after His resurrection).

Acts 2:38—"Then Peter said unto them, Repent, and be baptized everyone of you in the name of Jesus Christ for the remission of sins..."

Acts 10:43—"To Him give all the prophets witness, that through his name whosever believeth in Him shall receive remission of sins."

Romans 3:25—"Whom God hath set forth to be a propitiation through faith in His blood, to declare his righteousness for the remission of sins that are past, through the forbearance of God."

Hebrews 9:22—"...and without shedding of blood is no remission."

There are several hymns that contain references to remission (of sins) and/or forgiveness. "Your many sins are all forgiven, O hear the voice of Jesus" are words found in the "Great Physician" (Hunter/Stockton). "Would you be free from the burden of sin? There's power in the blood" are lyrics appearing in "There's Power in The Blood" (Jones/Jones). (The subtitle for this hymn when it was published in 1876 was "Without The Shedding Of Blood, There is No Remission of sin." Apparently, this subtitle was based on Hebrews 9:22).

The song, "Remission," has these lyrics: "The power of the cross shines from the sky. Remission of sins is shining bright" (album, Eternal, by Seventh Avenue). The lyrics, "Free from the law, Oh happy condition! Jesus hath bled, and there is remission" are found in the song, "Free From The Law—Oh Happy Condition."

REDEMPTION

Redemption refers to a payment that frees someone from an obligation, bondage (slavery), or danger. In a secular sense, the example of redemption that I have seen most frequently is that of a person who has to pay a fine for a traffic ticket whereupon a friend comes forward and pays the fine. Another example is a demand by kidnappers that unless a random is paid, the abducted person will not be released. Many Christian pastors and theologians use the terms "redemption" and "redeemed" interchangeably.

Of course, no matter the terminology, the important point to remember is that Jesus Christ paid the ultimate price, his death on the cross, for our sins so that we can escape from the penalty for them and be granted eternal salvation.

There are 11 references in the New Testament to "redemption," seven to "redeemed," two to "redeem," and none for "redeemer" or "redeemeth." In only one of thse verses do we find the words of Christ. In talking about the signs of this age, He said: "And when these things begin to pass, then look up, and lift up your heads; for your redemption draweth nigh" (Luke 21:28).

Luke 1:68 ("The Song Of Zacharias") refers to redemption: "Blessed be the Lord God of Israel; For He hath visited and redeemed His people." When Paul was prophesying about the coming of Jesus (Galatians 3:13), he said "Christ hath redeemed us from the curse of the law, being made a curse for us..."

There are three verses in Revelation that deal with redemption (5:9, 14:3, and 14:4)—all related to the end times and Jesus' second coming.

Representative verses for "Redemption" include Romans 3:24 ("Being justified freely by His grace through the redemption that is in Jesus Christ"), Ephesians 1:7 ("In whom we have redemption through His blood, the forgiveness of sins, according to the riches of His grace") and Ephesians 4:30 ("and grieve not the Holy Spirit of God, whereby ye are sealed unto the day of redemption").

Galatians 4:5 and Titus 2:14 contain the word "redeem": "To redeem them that were under the law, that we might receive the adoption of sons" (Galatians 4:5) and "who gave Himself for us, that He might redeem us from all iniquity" (Titus 2:14).

There are three verses in the New Testament that contain the word, "ransom." Two of these are utterances by Jesus: "Even as the Son of Man came not to be ministered to but to minister, and to give His life a ransom for many" Matthew 28:20. Mark 10:45 repeats (Matthew 28:20).

There is an interesting and informative reference to redemption in the Old Testament book of Ruth. Ruth and her mother-in-law, Naomi, left Moab for Israel. They were forced to undertake this journey because Naomi's son, Ruth's husband, Emilech, had died. Upon reaching Bethlehem, Boaz, a wealthy man who was a close relative ("kinsman") of Emilech's, showed kindness to Ruth by letting her glean his fields during harvest time. He eventually served in the role of kinsman-redeemer when he purchased (redeemed) a parcel of land that Naomi was entitled to and gave it to her. Boaz also purchased (redeemed) Ruth to be his wife. Obed, their son, gave birth to Jesse and Jesse gave birth to David, Israel's future king. If we follow the line of David to its conclusion (see Matthew 1:1-17) we find the name of the redeemer of all mankind, Jesus Christ.

There are many hymns that deal with the subject of redemption. Some of these are:

> "When I See The Blood" (John/J.G.F)—"Christ our redeemer died on the cross, Died for the sinner, Paid all his due."

> "There Is A Fountain Filled With Blood" (Cowper/ Mason)—"E'er since by faith I saw the stream… Redeeming love has been my theme."

> "Blessed Redeemer" (Christiansen/Loes)—"Blessed redeemer, precious redeemer, Seems now I see Him on Calvary's tree."

> "Redeemed" (Crosby/Kirkpatrick)—"Redeemed, How I love to proclaim it: Redeemed by the blood of the lamb."

> "Face To Face" (Breck/Tullar)—"Face to face with my redeemer, Jesus Christ who loves me so."

"Under His Wings" (Cushing/Sankey)—"Under his wings I am safely abiding, He has redeemed me, And I am His child."

"Nor Silver, Nor Gold" (Gray/Towner)—"Nor silver, nor gold hath obtained my redemption…But with a price, The blood of Jesus."

"Since I Have Been Redeemed" (Excell/Excell)—"I have a song I love to sing, Since I have been redeemed."

"He Lives on High" (McKinney/McKinney)—Christ the Savior came from Heaven's glory, To redeem the lost from sin and shame."

"I Know That My Redeemer Liveth" (Pounds/Fillmore)—" I know that my redeemer liveth, And on the earth again shall stand."

"The Great Redeemer" (Foster/Beazley)—"With what joy I tell the story of the love that makes men free, He has purchased my redemption."

Here are some of the hymns that refer to "ransom" or "ransomed":

"Saved By The Blood" (Henderson/Towner)—"Now ransomed from sin and a new work begun."

"My Redeemer" (Bliss/McCranahan)—"In His boundless love and mercy, He the ransom freely gave."

"All Hail The Power" (Perronet/Holden)—"Ye chosen seed of Israel's race, Ye ransomed from the fall."

"Now I Belong To Jesus" (Clatton/Clatton)—"He gave his life to ransom my soul, Not for the years of time alone, but for eternity."

"Give Of Your Best To The Master" (H. B. G./ Bamard)—"He gave Himself for your ransom. Give of your best to the master."

"All Hail, Immanuel" (Van Sickle/Gabriel)—"All hail to thee, Immanuel, The ransomed hosts surround Thee."

ATONEMENT

This is an aspect of salvation that can be best understood through an analysis of relevant passages found in the Old Testament, especially in Leviticus and Numbers. In all, there are around 80 references in the OT that pertain to atonement, only one in the New Testament. Romans 5:11 states: "And not only so, but we also joy in God through our Lord Jesus Christ, by whom we have now received the atonement." The note on this passage indicates that the noun form of"atonement" is "reconciled," which is found in Romans 5:10: "For if, when we were enemies, we were reconciled to God by the death of His Son, much more, being reconciled, we should be saved by His life."

Representative passages in the Old Testament that contain the word, "atonement," are:

Exodus 30:15—"The rich shall not give more, and the poor shall not give less than half a shekel, when they give an offering unto the Lord, to make an atonement for souls."

Exodus 32:30—"And it came to pass on the morrow, that Moses said unto the people; Ye have sinned a great sin and now I will go up unto the Lord, peradventure I shall make atonement for your sin." This was necessary because the Israelites had made a golden calf, worshipped it, and made sacrifices to it (see Exodus 32:8).

Leviticus 1:4—"And he shall put his hand upon the head of the burnt offering: and it shall be accepted for him to make atonement for him."

Leviticus 4:20—"And he shall do with the bullock as he did with the bullock for a sin offering, so shall he do with this: the priest shall make an atonement for them, and it shall be forgiven them."

Leviticus 5:6—"And he shall bring his trespass offering unto the Lord for his sin which he hath sinned, a female from the flock, a lamb or a kid of the goats for a sin offering; and the priest shall make an atonement for him concerning his sin."

Leviticus 9:7—"And Moses said unto Aaron, Go unto the altar and offer thy sin offering, and thy burnt offering, and make an atonement for thyself and for the people….and make an atonement for them; as the Lord hath commanded."

Numbers 8:19—"And I have given the Levites as a gift to Aaron and sons from among the children of Israel…and to make an atonement for the children of Israel."

Numbers 16:47—"And Aaron took as Moses commanded, and ran into the midst of the congregation; and behold, the plague was begun among the people: and he put on incense, and made an atonement for the people."

> Numbers 29:11-"One kid of the goats for a sin
> offering; beside the sin offering of atonement, and
> the continual burnt offering, and the meat offering
> of it, and their drink offerings.

There are several conclusions that are revealed by these passages about atonement. First, the term, "offering," suggests that there is some tangible action to be done by the supplicant in anticipation of being forgiven for his or her sins. Second, this offering often consisted of an animal being sacrificed; usually, these animals must be without blemish. The blood of these sacrificial animals is, of course, representative of the blood Jesus shed on the cross as atonement for our sins. Third, the sacrifices are usually made in conjunction with a request that sins be forgiven. Fourth, atonement can be offered to individuals or people, especially for the nation of Israel.

The Day of Atonement (Yom Kippur) is the most important Jewish holy day. Because its dates are linked to the Jewish calendar, the specific date on which it is celebrated will vary: October 11, 2016, September 29, 2017, for example.

Leviticus 16:29-30 summarizes the important aspects of the Day of Atonement: "And this shall be a statute forever unto you: that in the seventh month, on the tenth day of the month, ye shall afflict your souls and do no work at all...for on that day shall the priest make an atonement for you, to cleanse you that ye may be clean from all your sins before the Lord."

It is important to understand that the Day of Atonement deals only with the sins committed against God by INDIVIDUALS, and not those committed against God by the nation of Israel. It also does not deal with the sins of individuals committed against other individuals.

Another important aspect of the ceremony surrounding the Day of Atonement involves the high priest and two goats. The two goats were to be selected by lots. One goat was chosen for the Lord. It was slain as a sin offering to the Lord. On the second goat, the "scapegoat," the high priest laid his hand on its head, thereby transferring the sins of the people to it. Then, that goat was led away into the desert, signifying the removal of sin (Brand, Draper and English).

The writer believes that the scapegoat paints a vivid picture of Christ as the atonement for our sins. A scapegoat is someone or something that takes the blame—and the ensuing punishment—for sins and demands punishment for them so God had Jesus take on our sins and the accompanying punishment: death on the cross. All sins ever committed and future ones, as well, were piled on Jesus as he was crucified.

Below are the hymns the writer found that deal with atonement:

> "Rock Of Ages" (Toplady/Hastings)—"Could my tears forever flow, could my zeal no languor know, These for sin could not atone; Thou must save, and Thou alone".

> "I Won't Have To Cross Jordan Alone" (Ramsay/Durham)—"I won't have to cross Jordan alone.... Jesus died for my sins to atone."

> "Hallelujah For The Cross" (Bonar/McGranaham)— "Christ the blessed Son, Who did for sin atone."

PROPITIATION

There are three passage in the New Testament that contain the word, "propitiation." In Romans 3:25, Paul writes: "Whom God hath set forth to be a propitiation through faith in His blood, to declare His righteousness for the remission of sins that are past, through the forbearance of God." "And He is the propitiation for our sins: and not for ours only, but also for the sins of the whole world" (words of the apostle, John, in 1 John 2:2). This apostle also uses this word in 1 John 4:10: "Herein is love, not that we loved God, but that He loved us, and sent His Son to be the propitiation for our sins."

The notes on these three verses provide important perspectives on the concept of propitiation. The note on Romans 3:25 rephrased this verse, thusly: "Or, as the One who would turn away God's wrath, taking away all sin." The note on 1 John 2:2 says that propitiation refers to turning away God's wrath, God's wrath being caused by man's sin. By sending Jesus to make a substitutionary atonement for believers' sins, God's wrath is appeased, that is, propitiated. When discussing 1 John 4:10, the note refers the reader to the note on 1 John 2:2.

Leviticus 17:11 is an important Old Testament reference to propitiation: "God has given Israel the atonement to propitiate His wrath," that is, to appease it. (The atonement referred to in this verse is the blood of sacrificial animals which, of course, represents a type of Christ).

R. C. Sproul, in his book, "The Truth Of The Cross, "maintains that propitiation is the bringing about a change in God's attitude so that He is now with us, and no longer an enemy. He believes that propitiation is the object of expiation.

EXPIATION

Sproul defines expiation as taking away, or the removal of something, usually through the payment of a penalty or the offering of an atonement. In a religious sense, the something that is removed is guilt or sin.

In summary, propitiation and expiation involve a two-way flow, from God to man and from man back to God. That is, sin angers God, so he sent His Son to die for our sins (propitiation). When this gift results in sinners accepting Christ as their savior, God's wrath toward the former sinner is removed. Exhibit 3.2 diagrammatically illustrates the relationship between propitiation and expiation.

EXHIBIT 3.2
PROPITIATION AND EXPIATION

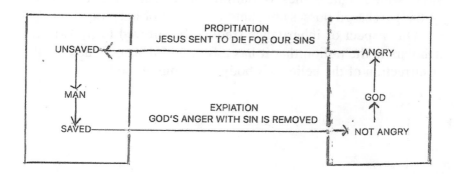

ADOPTION

When a sinner is born again, he or she becomes a son or daughter of God through adoption. Romans 8:15 says "For ye have not received the spirit of bondage to fear; but ye have received the spirit of adoption, whereby we cry, Abba, Father."

Adoption was never prevalent in Jewish society (an exception was Jacob adopting Joseph's two sons, Ephraim and Manasseh), but was a more common event in Roman and Greek cultures. One example was slaves being adopted by their masters (note the reference to "bondage" in Romans 8:15, a term often applied to a slave's relation to his or her master).

INHERITANCE

Romans 8:17 addresses an important aspects of adoption. As adoptees, we become heirs of God: "and if children, then heirs; heirs of God and joint heirs with Christ" As joint heirs with Christ, we and Christ become brothers and sisters, we through grace, Jesus as the son of God.

In Greek and Roman culture, a major benefit of being an heir was that an adopted son would be entitled to an inheritance. That believers, through adoption, are also entitled to an inheritance is captured in Colossians 3:24: "Knowing that of the Lord ye shall receive the reward of inheritance.." Ephesians 1:14, in following up on Ephesians 1:13, which refers to Christians believing in Jesus, says "which is the earnest of our inheritance, until the redemption of the purchased possession, unto the praise of his glory."

One aspect of inheritance frequently referred to by Biblical scholars is the notion that it has a future dimension, such as, the resurrection of the believer's body (see Youngblood).

CHAPTER FOUR

MAN'S PARTICIPATION
IN SALVATION

"For God so loved the world, that He gave his only begotten Son, that whosoever believeth in Him should not perish, but have everlasting life."

IN THE PREVIOUS CHAPTER, WE DEALT WITH 13 elements of salvation from God's perspective. In this chapter, we will approach the concept of salvation from man's perspective.

In Chapter Three, we placed these 13 components in a "wheel" to signify that they all essentially occur at the moment of salvation.

In Chapter Four, the reader will notice that we have put the four man-related dimensions of salvation in a flow chart (Exhibit 4.1) which makes the point, from man's point of view, that salvation is a process.

EXHIBIT 4.1
MAN'S PARTICIPATION
IN SALVATION

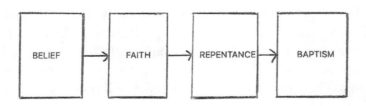

As each aspect of this process--belief, faith, repentance, and baptism--is discussed, a rationale for where each is placed in this model will be provided.

BELIEF

The writer is comfortable with placing belief as the starting point in the salvation process, followed immediately by faith. The following discussion, supported by appropriate Biblical verses, will support this sequence. Paul writes in 2 Timothy 1:2: "I know whom I have believed and am persuaded (faith) that He is able to keep what I have committed to Him until that day." Hebrews 11:6 states: "But without faith, it is impossible to please Him: For he that cometh to God must believe that He is and that He is a rewarder of them that diligently seek Him. The following verse (1 Peter 1:21) also supports the argument that faith follows belief: "Who by Him do BELIEVE in God, that raised Him up from the dead, and gave him glory, that your FAITH and hope might be in God." In Paul's letter (Romans: 10:17), we read: "So then faith cometh by hearing and hearing by the word of God."

Brand, Draper and England maintain that "The gospel must be heard and understood BEFORE FAITH CAN HAPPEN; faith occurs when someone moves through the words and the evidence and 'calls upon' or asks Christ to save" (emphasis added). They also write that recognition of need always precedes saving faith.

The number of times the words "believe," "believed", "believers," "believest," "believeth," and "believing" occur in the New Testament provides proof that belief is an important component of man's involvement in the salvation experience. "Belief" occurs 120 times. Fifty of these are found in John's gospel. Fifty-one of the 120 mentions are attributable to Jesus Christ.

The word "believed" appears 93 times, with 20 being uttered by Christ. The words "believers," "believest," "believeth"and "believing" occur twice, eight, 41, and eight times, respectively. The numbers attributed to Jesus are, respectively, zero, three, 18, and two. The author, in discussing belief will focus on what Jesus said, but will also refer to what is written by the various authors of books in the NT, especially those penned by Paul and Peter.

Some commentators consider that belief, faith and trust refer to the same concept. For example, Youngblood defines belief as "to place one's trust in God's truth—one who takes God at His word and trusts him for salvation." Brand, Draper and England, under the heading, Belief and Believe, refer the reader to the topic of faith, for which they devote about five pages of discussion.

While the author sees merit in the positions of these commentators, he feels that uncoupling belief and faith, as is done in Exhibit 4.1, will provide the reader with a more insightful understanding of God's gift of salvation.

It is enlightening to examine the lead definition of "believe" as found in the Smith's Bible Dictionary: "To credit upon the authority or testimony of another; to be persuaded of the truth of something upon the declaration of another, or upon evidence furnished by reasons, arguments and deductions of the mind, or by other circumstances than personal knowledge." In discussing this definition, this source says: "When we BELIEVE upon the authority of reasoning, arguments or a concurrence of facts and circumstances, we rest our conclusions upon their strength or probability, their agreements with our own experience, etc." (emphasis added). To be sure, this reference's statement suggests the concept of trust but does not intertwine belief and trust to the extent that Youngblood and Brand, Draper and England do. In fact, Brand, Draper and England, themseleves, strike a more uncoupled tone, more in line with the author's opinion, when they say: "The gospel must be heard and understood" (isn't this essentially "belief?") BEFORE faith can happen; faith occurs when someone moves THROUGH the words and evidence and 'calls upon' or asks Christ to save" (emphases added). This statement coincides with the author's opinion that in order to have faith, you first have to believe.

What does the Bible say man needs to believe in order to be saved? The scriptures below clearly indicate that belief, first, in Jesus is the key:

John 3:36: The apostle John said: "...he that believeth not on the Son shall not see life, but the wrath of God abideth in Him."

John 8:24: "For if ye believed not that I am He, ye shall die in your sins."

John 3:18: "he that believeth on Him is not condemned,"

John 7:31: When Jesus spoke in the temple, "many believed on Him."

Acts 16:31: "Believe on the Lord Jesus Christ and thou shalt be saved.."

Acts 19:4—"They should believe on Him which should come after Him."

John 3:16—"For God so loved the world that He gave his only begotten Son that whosoever believeth in Him shall not perish, but have everlasting life."

John 6:35—"I am the bread of life: he that cometh to Me shall never hunger; and he that believeth on me shall never thirst."

John 7:38: "He that believeth on Me, as the scripture hath said, out of his belly shall flow rivers of living water."

Romans 10:11—"For the scripture saith, whosoever believeth on Him shall not be ashamed."

Although the above verses clearly indicate that belief in Jesus is the key to being saved, there is none that specifically indicates WHAT WE NEED TO BELIEVE ABOUT HIM to be granted salvation. Fortunately, there are several verses in the NT that unequivocally answer this question. In Matthew 16:15, Jesus asked His disciples "But whom say ye that I am?" Peter replied (Matthew 16:16): "Thou art the Christ, the Son of the living God." Jesus responded: "Blessed art thou, Simon Barjona..."Thou art Peter, and upon this ROCK, I will build my church..."(emphasis added"). The Greek words for Peter and "rock" are quite similar; in this passage, rock refers to Peter's RESPONSE, not to Peter himself.

John 11:26-27 describes dialogue between Christ and Martha, the sister of Mary and Lazarus. John 11:26 said: "And whosever liveth and believeth in Me shall never die. Believest thou this?" Martha's reply was"..Yea, Lord: I believe that thou art the Christ, the Son of God, which should come into the world."

When the Ethiopian eunuch asked the apostle Philip—who was told by the angel of the Lord to rendezvous with the eunuch south of Jerusalem—why he could not be baptized, Philip told him: "If thou believest with all thine heart, thou mayst." The eunuch's response: "I believe that Jesus Christ is the Son of God" (Acts 8:36-37).

In Romans 4:22-24 Paul writes this about Abraham: "And therefore it was imputed to him for righteousness. Now, it was not written for his sake alone that it was imputed to him. But for us also, to whom it shall be inputed, if we believe on Him that raised up Jesus our Lord from the dead."

Paul writes in Romans 10:9, when discussing Jesus: "That if thou shall confess with thy mouth, and shall believe in thine heart that God hath raised Him from the dead, thou shall be saved."

POSITIVES OF BELIEF

Jesus' Words. Jesus had much to say about the positive outcomes for individuals who become saved by believing. Eight of these prouncements occur in the gospel of John. In John 3:15, Jesus told Nicodemus that "Whosoever believeth in Him should not perish but have everlasting life." Similar sentiments are contained in the favorite verse of many Christians: "For God so loved the world that He gave His only begotten Son, that whosoever believeth in Him should not perish but have everlasting life." (John

3:16) When Jesus addressed the people who sought Him out at Capernaum, He said: "..everyone which seeth the Son and believeth on Him may have everlasting life." During the last day of the Feast of Tabernacles Jesus, in the temple, said: "He that believeth on Me, as the scripture has said, out of his belly shall flow rivers of living water" (John 7:38). (The note on this verse equates "living water" with "eternal life").

When Jesus spoke to Martha and Mary, Lazarus' sisters, before he raised Lazarus from the dead, He said that her brother would rise again. When Martha responded that she knew he would be raised at the resurrection, Jesus told her: "I am the resurrection and the life: he that believeth in Me, though he were dead, yet shall live" (John 11:25). In John 12:46, Christ tells Andrew and Philip: "I am come a light in the world that whosoever believeth on me shall not abide in darkness."

John 14:12 contains these words of our Lord and Savior: "Verily, verily I say unto you, he that believeth on me, the works that I do shall he do also; and greater works than these shall he do…" Jesus uttered these words just prior to going to the cross.

The apostle Thomas (Didymus) said when the others had seen the risen Lord, that he would not believe until he saw a physical affirmation, such as, being able to put his finger into the prints of the nails. When actually doing this later, plus putting his hand into Jesus' side which had been pierced with a spear, Thomas indicated his belief by saying "My Lord and my God." Jesus replied: "Thomas, because thou hast seen me, thou hast believed: blessed are they that have not seen, and yet have believed" (John 20:29).

Words Of Others. Other New Testament scriptures, mainly those of the apostles, confirm Jesus' statements about the benefits from salvation for believers:

> Romans 1:16—Paul, in his letter to the Romans, states: For I am not ashamed of the gospel of God unto salvation to everyone that believeth; to the Jew first and also to the Greek."

Romans 9:33—When indicating that the gospel was available to the Jews, Paul said: "As it is written, Behold I lay in Sion a stumbling stone and rock of offence: and whosoever believeth on Him shall not be ashamed."

1 John 5:1, the apostle John maintains "whosoever believes that Jesus is the Christ is born of God..."

1 John 5:10—The apostle, John, maintains in this verse: "He that believeth on the Son of God hath the witness in himself..."

The above verses confirm that the most important positive of belief in Jesus is eternal life. Others mentioned are not being in darkness, able to do good works, belief in Jesus without having seen Him, no shame, and having the indwelling of the Holy Spirit ("hath the witness").

NEGATIVES RESULTING FROM NON-BELIEF

Jesus' Words. Previously, we indicated what the positives are of belief in Jesus. It is only logical that we also need to see what the negatives of non-belief are. We will first examine what Jesus had to say.

After His resurrection, He appeared to His apostles while they ate and "upbraided them with their unbelief and hardness of heart, because they believed not them that had seem Him after He was risen" (Mark 16:14). In John 3:18, we find these words of our Lord and Savior: "He that believeth on Him is not condemned: but he that believeth not is condemned already because he hath not believed in the name of the only begotten Son of God." "I said therefore unto you, that ye shall die in your sins: for if ye believe not that I am He, ye shall die in your sins" (Jesus' words directed to the Pharisees, John 8:24). Mark 16:16 contains these words of our Lord and Savior: "...but he that believeth not shall be damned" (Jesus' conversation with Nicodemus).

In summary, these passages indicate that non-believers will die, be damned, reproved, condemned, and be the target of God's wrath.

Words Of Others. Below are some scriptures that contain indications by others than Jesus that identify the negative consequences of non-belief.

2 Thessalonians 2:11-12—Paul, preaching in Thessalonika, said "That they all might be damned who believeth not the truth, but had pleasure in unrightousness." (The note on this verse said that it applies to those who do not belive in Christ but, instead, believe in the Anti Christ).

Hebrews 3:18-19—The writer maintains that those who do not believe will not enter into rest as will those who are believers.

2 Corinthians 4:4—In this second of Paul's letters to believers in Corinth, he maintains that Satan has blinded the minds of those who "believed not," which prevents them from having the glorious gospel of Christ shining on them.

John 3:36—The apostle John writes that"...he that believeth not the Son shall not see life; but the wrath of God abideth on him."

The consequences of not believing, according to the above scriptures, are positively frightening. Consider the words used to condemn unbelievers: damned, would get no rest, would be blind about the gospel, will not receive salvation, and will see the wrath of God.

ANSWERS TO SPECIFIC QUESTIONS ABOUT SALVATION

There are several instances in the New Testament where people specifically asked what they needed to do to be saved. As we will see, belief appears to be the key factor.

Acts 16:25-32 describes an event that occurred when Paul and Silas were imprisoned in Philippi. While they were praying and singing praises to God, a great earthquake occurred, causing the cell doors to be opened and they and other prisoners were loosed from their stocks. The chief jailer became distraught, fearing all of the prisoners would escape. Paul and Silas, however, made no effort to get away. Falling down before them, he asked, "Sirs, what must I do to be saved?" Paul and Silas responded, "BELIEVE on the Lord Jesus Christ and thou shalt be saved, and thy house" (emphasis added).

When the people took ships across the Sea and Galilee in search of Jesus, they asked Him, "What shall we do that we might work the works of God?" Jesus responded, "Tis is the work of God, that ye BELIEVE on Him whom He sent" (John 6:28-29) (emphasis added). The note indicates that the people were thinking that their pious works would achieve for them everlasting life. Jesus' response corrected this misconception.

John 9:1-12 describes Jesus healing a blind man. Later (John 9:37), Jesus asked the blind man, "Does thou BELIEVE on the Son of God?" The blind man asked "Who is he, Lord, that I might BELIEVE on him?" Jesus said, "Thou hast seen Him and it is He that talketh with thee." The blind man responded, I BELIEVE. And he worshipped Him" (emphases added).

There are many hymns that have references to belief. The hymn. "I Know Whom I Have Believed" (Nathan/McGranaham) contains this chorus: "But I know whom I have believed, and am persuaded that He is able to keep that which I've committed unto Him against that day."

Some hymns that deal with belief contain promises pertinent to those who have believed. The hymn, "Verily, Verily" (McGranaham) states "He that believeth on the Son saith He Hath everlasting life." The song by Fanny Crosby and W.H. Doane, "To God Be The

Glory," also provides a favorable outcome of believing: "A perfect redemption, the purchase of blood, to every believer, the promise of God." Another promise is found in W.A. Ogden's hymn, "Look And Live": "I will tell you I came, Hallelujah, to Jesus When He made me whole, 'Twas believing on His name, hallelujah, I trusted and He saved my soul." Another promise is contained in "Only Trust Him (Stockton): "Believe in Him without delay, and you are fully blest." Fanny Crosby and George C. Stebbins, in their hymn, "Jesus is Calling," point to the happiness that follows belief: "They who believe on His name shall rejoice."

The popular song, "I Believe," introduced in 1953 and sung by such luminaries as Elvis Presley and Frankie Laine (composers: Styne, Drake, Stillman, Shirl, and Graham), contains these lyrics:

"I believe for everyone who goes astray,
Someone will come to show the way
I believe, I believe."
"I believe above the storm the smallest prayer will still be heard..
Then I know why, I believe."

FAITH

Let's examine the scriptures in light of what they have to say about faith. (There are about 230 references to "faith" in the NT, 2 by Jesus) In doing so, our focus will be on those that deal with the concept of salvation. We are not concerned with those that address the idea of faith after a person is saved, nor those that describe the relationship of faith in performing miracles, such as, healing people who are blind, lame, afflicted with leprosy, and so on.

It seems logical that faith should be subsequent to belief in the man-oriented aspect of salvation and should precede repentance. Once a person believes what is required to achieve salvation, he or she needs to confirm this belief with the faith that God will deliver the promises made to believers.

JESUS' WORDS

When Paul was confronted by Jesus on the way to Damascus, He was told that he was to be a witness to the Gentiles. In elaborating on this revelation, our Lord and Savior said: "To open their eyes, and to turn them from darkness to light, and from the power of Satan unto God: that they may receive forgiveness of sins, and inheritance among the which are sanctified by FAITH that is in me" (Acts 26:18, emphasis added).

In Revelation 2:10, we note these words of Jesus as he was speaking to the church at Smyrna: "..be thou FAITHFUL unto death, and I will give thee a crown of life" (emphasis added).

WORDS OF THE APOSTLES

The apostles, chiefly Paul, frequently made statements about faith. The following demonstrate (1) the importance of faith in the salvation process and (2) how intertwined faith is with the 13 God-related aspects of salvation discussed in the previous chapter.

In Paul's letter to the Romans (1:17), he wrote: "For therein is the RIGHTEOUSNESS of God revealed from FAITH to FAITH as it is written the just shall live by FAITH" (emphases added). In Romans 3:28 he said: "Therefore, we conclude that a man is JUSTIFIED by FAITH without the deeds of the law" (emphases added). The apostle writes in Romans 3:25 that "whom God hath set forth to be a PROPITIATION through FAITH in His blood to declare His RIGHTEOUSNESS for the remission of sins...". His comments in Romans 3:31 are instructive: "Do we then make void the law through FAITH? God forbid: yea, we establish the law" (emphasis added).

Four additional utterances by this apostle occur in Romans. In Romans 4:13, we find these words: "For the promise that He should be the heir of the world, was not to Abraham, or to his seed, through the law, but through the RIGHTEOUSNESS of FAITH (emphases added). Romans 4:16 contains this statement: "Therefore, it is of FAITH, that it might be by grace; to the end the promise might be sure to all the seed, not to that only which is of the law; but to that also which is the FAITH of Abraham; who is the father of us all" (emphasis added).

Paul also said, "Therefore being JUSTIFIED by FAITH, we have peace with God through our Lord Jesus Christ" (Romans 5:1, emphases added). In Romans 9:30, when Paul stated that the gospel needed to be offered to the Jews, he first said this about the Gentiles: "What shall we say then? That the Gentiles, which followed not after RIGHTEOUSNESS have attained to RIGHTEOUSNESS even the RIGHTEOUSNESS which is of FAITH (emphases added),

In Galatians 2:16, Paul, writing in opposition to Peter, argued that saved Gentiles did not need to live as Jews: "Knowing that a man is NOT JUSTIFIED by the works of the law, but by the FAITH of Jesus Christ" (emphases added). (The note on this passage says: "FAITH is the means by which JUSTIFICATON is received..."). In Galatians 3:8, Paul writes: "And the scriptures, forseeing that God would JUSTIFY the heathen through FAITH.." (emphases added).

In Galatians 3:22, we find these words of Paul: "But the scripture, foreseeing that God would JUSTIFY the heathen through FAITH..." (emphases added). Galatians 5:5 offers these words penned by Paul: "For we through the Spirit wait for the hope of RIGHTEOUSNESS through FAITH (emphasis added). The well-known Ephesians 2:8 states "For by grace are ye saved through FAITH" (emphasis added). Philippians 3:9 talks about the "RIGHTEOUSNESS of God by FAITH" (emphasis added).

The lyrics of some hymns deal with the faith aspect of salvation. As was done with belief, the focus will be chiefly on those that are related to the salvation process.

"Faith Of Our Fathers" (Faber/Hemy) contains these lyrics: "Faith of our fathers! Living still in spite of dungeon, fire and sword." "His faithful follower I would be, For by His hand He leadeth me" are part of the refrain found in "He Leadeth Me" (Gilmore/Bradbury). "How Firm A Foundation" (Keith/Steele) informs us: "How firm a foundation, ye saints of the Lord, is laid for your faith in His excellent word." The refrain of "Living By Faith" (Wells/Heath) deals with the notion of faith as follows: "Living by faith in Jesus above, Trusting, confiding in His great love."

The first line in "O For A Faith That Will Not Shrink" (Bathurst/ Dykes) repeats the title, then adds "Tho' pressed by every foe." "There Is A Fountain Filled With Blood" (Cowper/Mason) reminds us: "E'er since, by faith, I saw the stream, Thy flowing wounds supply." The fourth verse of "It Is Well With My Soul" (Spafford/ Bliss) begins with these lyrics: "And, Lord, haste the day when the faith shall be sight, The clouds be rolled back as a scroll."

REPENTANCE

There are various definitions of repentance that are found in the major reference sources consulted by the author. While there is a great deal of similarity in them, the author was surprised that there was not a greater level of conformity regarding this integral element of the man-related aspect of salvation.

Brand, Draper and England define repentance as a "deeply seated and thorough turning to God." They go on to say that "it occurs when a radical turning to God takes place, an experience in which God is recognized as the most important fact of one's existence."

Youngblood defines repentance as a change of mind or a feeling of remorse or regret for past conduct. True repentance is a "godly sorrow for sin, an act of turning around and going in the opposite direction." Youngblood emphasizes the idea of being sorry which the author believes is a key aspect of repentance, but is not explicitly contained in the definition provided by Brand, Draper and England.

Youngblood asserts that repentance and faith are "two sides of the same coin, that is, repentance represents the believer's turning away from sin, whereas faith refers to a turning toward God when Jesus Christ is accepted as Lord and Savior.

Repentance involves both an intellectual component and a heart component. Youngblood states that repentance is associated with prayer (1 Kings 8:47), belief (Mark 1:15), baptism (Acts 2:38), and conversion (Acts 3:19). Believers may repent because they have wronged God, a person, or a thing.

While repentance is part of the process of salvation, it should be noted that believers are expected to continually repent of sins they have committed as believers <u>after being saved</u> by asking God for forgiveness (see Revelation 2:5, 16-21, 22, and 3:3, 19). This assertion parallels the author's opinion that for many believers, the level of repentance they have about sins committed prior to being saved become greater after salvation because the indwelling of the Holy Spirit makes the believer even more conscious of the gravity of these sins and, consequently, even more appreciative of God's grace.

There are a total of 66 references to "Repent," "Repentance" "Repented," and "Repenteth" in the new testament. Twenty-seven contain Jesus' words.

JESUS AND REPENTANCE

There are several verses that reveal what Jesus had to say about repentance as it is related to salvation. When the Pharisees remonstrated Him for eating with publicans and sinners, He said: "I came not to call the righteous, but sinners to repentance" (Mark 2:17). In Luke 15:10, as he engaged the Pharisees and scribes via the parable of the Lost Sheep, He said: "Likewise, I say unto you, there is joy in the presence of the angels of God over one sinner that repenteth."

When Christ began His ministry in Gailee, He said: "Repent for the kingdom of Heaven is at hand" (Matthew 4:17). In Mark 1:15, our Lord said: "The time is fulfilled and the kingdom of God is at hand: repent ye, and believe the gospel." As our Lord spoke to His disciples and a multitude of people, He issued this somber warning: "I tell you, nay: but except you repent, ye shall also likewise perish" (Luke 13:3). In Matthew 11:20, Jesus upbraided the cities where most of His mighty works were done because "they repenteth not." The Lord identified Chorazin, Bethsaida and Capernaum as the guility ones (Matthew 11:21-23).

JESUS' DISCIPLES AND REPENTANCE

Following are some of the passages alluding to Jesus' disciples and repentance. When Christ urged His disciples to witness, "they went out, and preached that men should repent" (Mark 6:12). In Acts 3:19, during Peter's sermon in the temple, he said: "Repent ye therefore, and be converted, that your sins may be blotted out..." Mark 1:4 refers to John the Baptist's ministry: "John did baptize in the wilderness and preach the baptism of repentance for the remission of sins." Paul observed in Romans 2:4: "...not knowing that the goodness of God leadeth thee to repentance." The note to this verse says "The purpose of God's kindness is to give opportunity for repentance." Second Peter 3:9 has this to say about repentance: "The Lord...is not willing that any should perish, but that all should come to repentance."

Following are the titles and lyrics of two hymns that refer to repentance. "Victory In Jesus" (Bartlett), one of the author's favorites, contains these lyrics: "I heard about His groaning, of His precious blood atoning, Then I repented of my sins and won the victory." The hymn, "Lord, I'm Coming Home" (Kirkpatrick), contains the following lyrics: I've wasted precious years, Now I'm coming home; I now repent with bitter tears, Lord, I'm coming home."

BAPTISM

The reader will notice that baptism has been placed at the end of the salvation-from-man's perspective. This was done for several reasons. Baptism is essentially a profession by the believer that he has already accepted Jesus Christ as his Lord and Savior. Baptism is often viewed as an overview representation of salvation, that is, the sinner, his death because of sin, and everlasting life as represented by resurrection: the person in the water (the sinner), his death because of sin (submerged), and everlasting life/resurrection (coming up out of the water to escape death). The note on Mark 1:4, which describes John the Baptist baptizing in the wilderness, supports placing baptism at the end of the salvation process (from man's perspective): "John was preaching repentance-baptism," that is, the writers most likely felt that baptism follows repentance.

Some churches believe that baptism actually is the means by which people are saved. This cannot be the case because allowing oneself to be baptized is an act of man's, whereas, salvation is solely a gift from God (see Brand, Draper and England). The note to Romans 6:3-4 is more direct: "Baptism is not a means whereby we enter into a vital faith with Jesus Christ..."

Probably the most significant utterance by Jesus regarding baptism is found in Mark 16:16. When Jesus, after his resurrection, was taking to his disciples, He said: "He that believeth and is baptized shall be saved, but he believeth not shall be damned." The note accompanying this passage is instructive: "Baptism does not save, nor is it required for salvation. Notice that in order to be 'damned,' one has only not to believe. Nothing is said about not being baptized." The repentant thief crucified with Jesus could not be baptized but was told by Jesus that he would be with Him in paradise that very day (Luke 33:32).

A question often asked about baptism is who can be baptized? The obvious answer is anyone who has made a sincere statement of faith in Jesus Christ. Some churches believe in the doctrine of infant baptism, declaring that through this procedure, the child will be saved. This, of course, is fallacious thinking because the child is not old enough to make a statement of faith; indeed, there is no mention in the New Testament of infants being baptized (Youngblood.) A better take on infant baptism is that it serves as a commitment by the parents to provide a Christian environment so that the baptized infant, when older, will be saved.

This reservation concerning infant baptism is not meant to suggest that children CAN'T be saved and, then, baptized. The author has witnessed in his own church many baptisms of six, seven, and eight year olds.

Another question is when should a person baptized. The answer is as soon as possible after being saved. (Don't forget that the Ethiopian eunuch in Acts 8:36-38 said "why not now?"). If, for various reasons, it may not be possible for new Christians to be baptized immediately after being saved, it should be done later when the circumstances will be more supportive.

Another question is what type of baptism is appropriate? The options are sprinkling, dousing, or total immersion. Because total immersion is most representative of the conversion process, it is preferred, but the other options are acceptable, especially when there is not a bapestry or body of water available.

There are 19 mentions by Christ of baptism in the New Testament. There is a total of 88 references to "Baptism," "Baptize," and "Baptized;" some are duplicates. In four verses (Matthew 20-23, Mark 10:38-39, Mark 11:30, and Luke 20:4), Jesus uses the notion of baptism to describe the agony on the cross He would have to endure. In Matthew 20-24 and Mark 10:38-39, Jesus deals with the desire of the mother of the apostles, James and John, that they be seated in Heaven on Jesus' right and left sides. Jesus' response: "Ye know not what ye ask: Are ye able to drink of the cup that I shall drink of and to be baptized with the baptism that I am baptized with?" Essentially, the same words appear in Mark 10:38-39. In talking with Peter (Luke 12:50), our Lord expresses the same sentiment: "But I have a baptism to be baptized with." The accompanying note says "that this 'baptism' refers to the suffering that Jesus was to endure on the cross."

In Mark 11:30 and Luke 20:4—in a confrontation with the chief preists, scribes and elders—Jesus asked: "The baptism of John, was it from Heaven or of men? Answer Me." Jesus knew that whatever answer they gave, it would be viewed as being fallacious.

Below are the lyrics to four hymns that contain allusions to baptism:

> "Baptized In Water" (Michael A. Seaward)— "Baptized in water, Sealed by the spirit, cleansed by the blood of Christ, our King."

> "Christ, When For Us You Were Baptized" (Bland/Tucker)—"Christ, when for us you were baptized, God's spirit on You came...Baptize with your spirit, Lord."

"Lord, When You Came To Jordan" (Wren)—"Lord, bring to us our Jordan, of newly opened eyes..As you were baptized."

"Down To The Sacred Wave" (Smith/Woodman)— "Down to the sacred wave, The Lord of life was led; and He who came our souls to save, In Jordan bowed His Head."

CHAPTER FIVE

GOD'S PROMISES TO SAVED PEOPLE

"Standing on the promises that can not fail, When the howling storms of doubt and fear assail" "Standing On The Promises" (Carter/Carter).

GOD HAS MADE A NUMBER OF PROMISES TO people who have been saved. (See front cover). These are not conditional, that is, there is nothing that saved people have to do to receive them. Recognizing that Jesus Christ is Lord and Savior is sufficient. Additionally, God will not renege on these promises no matter what sin a believer commits after being born again.

ETERNAL LIFE—IN HEAVEN

There are numerous passages in the New Testament that clearly reveal that a saved individual is granted eternal life. Below are some of the most unequivocal and powerful indications of this promise:

1. John 3:16—"For God so loved the world that he gave his only begotten Son that whosoever believeth on Him should not perish but have everlasting life." (Jesus' words).
2. John 3:15—"That whosoever believeth in Him should not perish but have eternal life." (Jesus' words).

3. John 6:47—"Verily, verily I say unto you, he that belie-veth on Me hath everlasting life." (Jesus' words). The word, "verily," denotes emphasis. Jesus' uttering it twice signifies additional emphasis.
4. John 11:26—"And whosoever liveth and believeth in Me shall neveral die." (Jesus' words, spoken to Martha, Lazarus' sister, before our Lord raised Lazarus from the dead).
5. 1 John 5:13—"These things have I written unto you that believe on the name of the Son of God; that ye may know that ye have eternal life..." (Words of the apostle John).
6. John 5:24—"Verily, verily, I say unto you, He that heareth my word, and believeth on Him that sent Me, hath ever-lasting life..." (Jesus' words).

As a saved individual, we are promised that we will live in Heaven (or the kingdom of God, or paradise) after we physically die. The proof texts are:
1. Mark 10:15—"Verily, I say unto you, whosoever shall not receive the kingdom of God as a little child, he shall not enter therein" (Jesus' words).
2. John 3:3—"Verily, verily, I say unto thee, except a man be born again, he cannot see the kingdom of God" (Jesus' words).
3. John 3:5—"Verily, verily, I say unto thee: except a man be born of water and the Spirit, he cannot enter into the kingdom of God" (Jesus' words).
4. 2 Corinthians 5:1—"For we know that if our earthly house of this tabernacle were dissolved, we have a building of God, a house not made with hand, eternal in the heavens" (words of the apostle, John).
5. Luke 23:43—When talking to the repentant thief on the cross, Jesus said: "Verily, I say unto thee, Today shalt thou be with me in paradise."
6. 2 Corinthians 5:5—"To an inheritance incorruptible and undefiled, and that fadeth not away, reserved in heaven for you" (Peter's words).

There are several hymns that remind Christians that they will go to heaven. "There Is A Green Hill Far Away (Alexander/Stebbins) that says: "That we might go at last to heaven, Saved by His precious blood." "Love Divine" (Wesley/Zundel) reads "Till in heaven we take our place." "When we all get to heaven, what a day of rejoicing that will be" are lyrics contained in "When We All Get To Heaven" (Hewitt/Wilson). The words, "When by the gift of His infinite grace, I am accorded in heaven a place," are found in "O That Will Be Glory For Me" (Gabriel/Gabriel).

There are two aspects of Jesus that believers in heaven can look forward to. We will see Jesus face to face. The hymn, "Face To Face" (Breck/Tullar) indicates "Face to face with my Redeemer, Jesus Christ who loves me so." "And some day I shall see Hm face to face" are words found in the hymn, "Jesus Is The Sweetest Name I Know" (Long). "My Savior First Of All" (Crosby/Sweney) states: "And His smile will be the first to welcome me." "Nothing Between" (Tindle/Clark) says "Nothing between my soul and the Savior, So that His blessed face may be seen."

Bromiley states that seeing God face to face is reserved for believers in the life to come. He alludes to 1 Corinthians 13:12 to support this assertion: "For now we see through a glass darkly but then face to face." In discussing the rapture (more about this later). 1 Thessalonians 4:17 says: "Then we which are alive and remain shall be caught up together with them in the clouds, to meet the Lord in the air: and so shall we ever be with the Lord."

We will also be with Jesus forever. 1 Corinthians 5:10 says: "Who died for us, that ... we should live together with Him. "And if I go and prepare a place for you, I will come again, and receive you unto myself; that where I am, that ye may be also." (See John 14:3).

Several hymns allude to our being with Jesus forever. "Some day I'll reach the golden shore and dwell with Jesus ever more" are lyrics found in "Some Day, It Won't Be Long" (Bridgers/Bridgers). "Christ Arose" (Lowry/Lowry) says: "Up from the grave He arose, With a mighty triump o'er His foes, And He lives forever with His saints to reign."

MANSIONS IN HEAVEN

"When We All Get To Heaven" (Hewitt/Wilson) states: "In the mansions bright and blessed, He'll prepare for us a place." "Beulah Land" (Stites/Sweney) has these lyrics: "I look across the sea where mansions are prepared for me." A similar promise is found in "Mansions Over The Hilltop" (Stanfill/Stanfill): "I've got a mansions just over the hilltop." "Victory In Jesus" (Bartlett/Bartlett) has these words: "I heard about a mansion He has built for me in glory." The hymn, "I Feel Like Traveling On" (Humber/Vaughan), promises: "My heavenly one is bright and fair, That heavenly mansion shall be mine."

Of course, the Bibical support for the notion of mansions in heaven being reserved for believers is found in Jesus' words (John 14:2): In my Father's house are many mansions: If it were not so, I would have told you. I go to prepare a place for you."

THE NEW JERUSALEM

There will be a holy city, New Jerusalem, that will come down from heaven and will be the "eternal dwelling place of the faithful" (Revelation 21:15, note). Its wall was of jasper, the city was of pure gold, like clear glass (Revelation 21:18). The foundation of the city was "garnished with all manner of precious stones," twelve of them (Revelation 21:19-20). The city's twelve gates were made of pearls.

The city had no need for the sun or the moon due to the presence of the glory of God and the light of the Lamb (Revelation 21:22). There will be no temple in the city because the Lord God almighty and the Lamb are there (Revelation 21:22).

From the throne of God there will flow the "water of life, clear as crystal" (Revelation 22:1). The tree of life will be there; it will bear 12 types of fruit every month. And its leaves will be for the healing of the nations (Revelation 22:1-2).

BELIEVERS WILL RECEIVE A NEW NAME

Revelation 2:17 reveals that Jesus will give a new name to all believers: "To him that overcometh will I give...a white stone, and in the stone a new name written."

Isaiah 62:2 is also relevant: "And the Gentiles which shall see Thy righteousness...and thou shalt be called by a new name, which the mouth of the Lord shall name." The hymn, "A New Name In Glory" (Miles/Miles), alludes to this gift: "There's a new name written down in glory, And it's mine, O yes it's mine." The hymn, "Holy Spirit, Faithful Guide" (Wells/Wells), contains these lyrics: "Looking up to heaven in prayer, Joyful that our names are there."

WHO WILL KNOW THE NEW NAME?

There is an intriguing element of this promise: No one will know the new name except the person who has been given it by Jesus Christ. Once again, we refer to Revelation 2:17: "To him that overcometh, will I give him a white stone and in the stone a new name written, which NO MAN KNOWETH SAVING HE THAT RECEIVETH IT" (emphasis added). Interestingly, Revelation 19:12, in describing Jesus' second coming, says that He will have a witten name "that no man knew, but He himself."

WHAT WILL BE THE BASIS FOR THE NEW NAME?

It is likely that this new name for believers will be a manifestation of an individual's physical appearance, circumstance, or behavior, past or present. Esau's name meant "hairy," Moses's name meant "drawn out of the water," and Jacob's meant "supplanter" because he stole Esau's birthright. The angel told Joseph to name his son, "Jesus," because Jesus would save his people from their sins. Peter's name means "rock," because he would become steadfast in supporting Jesus.

WHERE ELSE WILL BELIEVERS' NAMES BE WRITTEN DOWN?

Besides on a stone, where else might the believer's name be written down? Revelation 3.5 provides the answer: "He that over-cometh, the same shall be clothed in white raiment and I will not blot out his name out of the book of life." In discussing the perse-cution of Earth's people by the Anti Christ, Revelation 13:8 says: "And all that dwell upon the Earth shall worship him, whose names are not written in the book of life of the Lamb."

When the 70 apostles were commissioned by Jesus, He told them not to rejoice because they claimed that devils were sub-ject to them but, rather, that their names were written in heaven (Luke 10:20).

WILL WE SEE OUR LOVED ONES IN HEAVEN?

Many hymns describe the reunion in heaven with our loved ones who are already there. "Some Day, It Won't Be Long" (Bridgers/ Bridgers) has these words: "Some day I'll reach the golden shore... I'll meet the ones who have gone before." We Shall See The King Someday (Jones/Jones) contains these lyrics: "There with all the loved ones who have gone before, We shall the King some day." "I have a loving mother up in glory land...She's waiting for me in heaven's open door" — words found in "This World Is Not My Home" (Brumley). "The Sweet By and By" says: "In the sweet by and by, We will meet on that beautiful shore" (Bennett/Webster). The hymn, "Where We'll Never Grow Old" (Moore/Moore), has these lyrics: "And our voices will blend with the loved ones who have gone before." "God be with you 'till we meet again... 'till we meet at Jesus' feet" are lyrics appearing in the hymn, "God Be With You" (Rankin/Tomer). The song, "Hallelujah, We Shall Rise," contains these words: "When our fathers and our mothers and our loved ones, We shall see, In the resurrection morning." "When The Mists Have Rolled Away" (Herbert/Sankey) states: "We shall gather 'round the throne, Face to face with those who love us."

A special consideration is will believers be united in heaven with their children who have died before they have? It is likely that this will be an important question for parents who have prematurely lost children because many people, including pastors, have said that nothing in life is more traumatic than this event. The comment that the bereaving parents often utter is "it's not supposed to happen this way; we are supposed to outlive our children."

Pastor Donald Grey Barnhouse, in his book, "The Invisible War," states emphatically: that God's love should bring comfort, courage and hope to parents who have lost children: "THEY CAN NEVER LOSE THEIR CHILDREN" (emphasis added). "They may go to the cemetery and see the casket containing their remains lowered into the ground, but the loved ones who have gone are still the children of their parents."

Barnhouse's argument is based on his astute analysis of the Old Testament book of Job. Job's possessions consisted of 10 children (seven sons and three daughters), 7,000 sheep, 3,000 camels, 500 yoke of oxen, and 500 she asses. All of these were taken from him through a series of natural disasters. At the end of this book, God restoreth to Job 14,000 sheep, 6,000 camels, 1,000 yoke of oxen, 1,000 she asses, and 10 children (seven sons and three daughters).

Except for the children, Job was given twice as many of his original possessions. Because, in actuality, Job now had 20 childen (14 sons and six daughters) — 10 on earth and 10 in heaven, "where Job would meet them in the morning."

Barnhouse concludes his discussion by stating: "That is true for everyone who has lost a child. Our loved ones are safe in His keeping. If you have four children and one dies, never say that you now have three children. Say that you have four and that ONE OF THEM HAS GONE TO HEAVEN" (emphasis added).

There is a significant verse in Acts 16:16-34 that suggests that a believer's children will also be in heaven. Paul said to the jailer: "Believe on the Lord Jesus Christ, and thou shalt be saved, AND THY HOUSE" (emphasis added). Acts 16:34 indicates the jailer brought Paul and Silas into his house, "set meat before them, and rejoiced, believing in God WITH ALL HIS HOUSE" (emphasis added).

CROWNS

A number of hymns allude to the fact that when believers get to heaven, we will be allowed to wear crowns. "Saved Through Jesus' Blood" (Van de Venter/Van de Venter) says: I'll then receive a bright and starry crown, When after standing before the judgment bar." "To him that overcometh, God giveth a crown" is found in the hymn, "Yield Not To Temptation" (Palmer/Palmer). "Must Jesus Bear The Cross Alone?" (Shepherd/Allen) refers to crowns thusly: "And then go home my crown to wear, For there's a crown for me." The lyrics of "Fairest Lord Jesus" (Willis) say "Thou art my soul's glory, joy and crown." "Holy, Holy, Holy" (Hebner/Dikes) alludes to the type of crowns: "All The Saints adore Thee, Casting down their golden crowns around the glassy sea."

There are many Biblical passages that clearly indicate that believers in heaven will be adorned with crowns:

1. 2 Timothy 4:8—"Henceforth, there is laid up for me a crown of righteousness, which the Lord, the righteous judge, shall give me at that day: and not to me only, but unto all them also that love His appearing" (words of the apostle, Paul). (The note on this passage says "that day" refers to the second coming of Jesus Christ).
2. 1 Peter 5:4—"And when the chief shepherd shall appear, Ye shall receive a crown of glory that fadeth not away."
3. James 2:1-2—"Blessed is the man that endureth temptation: for when he is tried, he shall receive the crown of life, which the Lord hath promised to them that love Him."
4. Revelation 2:10—"Be thou faithful unto death, and I will give thee a crown of life" (Jesus' words).

What do crowns represent? The Aid To Bible Understanding maintains that after the flood, crowns represent authority, dignity, honor, power, and rewards for faithfulness. Smith contends that we receive an imperishable crown as a reward for our faithfulness. Holman states that crowns symbolize power, most importantly, a "Crown of Life" represents eternal life (see note on James 1:12).

Revelation 4:4 describes a scene in heaven involving 24 elders who sit in 24 seats around the throne of God. On their heads, they wear "crowns of gold." The number 24 is often used to denote the 12 tribes of Israel plus the 12 apostles (see note).

GARMENTS

The hymn, "The Home Over There," indicates the type of garments that the saved will wear in heaven: "Where the saints...are robed in their garments of white."

Passages in Revelation confirm and elaborate on these lyrics. "And white robes were given unto every one of them" (Revelation 6:11). "Them" refers to the saints who were martyred during the great tribulation brought about by the Anti Christ. Revelation 7:9 says"...a great multitude....stood before the throne, and before the Lamb, clothed with white robes..." Revelation 3:5 says "He that overcometh, the same shall be clothed in white raiment; and I will not blot his name out of the book of life..." (Jesus' words). (The note on this passage says that an "overcomer" is "every Christian, every believer").

Revelation 19:14 states "And the armies which were in heaven followed Him upon white horses, clothed in fine linen, white and clean." (The note on this passage says that these robes adorn the redeemed church).

A FEAST

Several hymns refer to a glorious feast that the elect will have with Jesus Christ Himself. The hymn, "Come And Dine" (Widmeyer/Bolton) contains these lyrics: "Jesus has a table spread, where the saints of God are fed." "Lo, the table is spread and the feast is waiting there" are lyrics found in the hymn, "Calling The Prodigal" (Gabriel/Gabriel).

A Biblical passage about this feast is found in Revelations 19:9 which states "Blessed are they which are called unto the marriage supper of the Lamb."

A NEW BODY

When Christians get to heaven, they will be given a new body. This body will be spiritual. Thus, our new body will no longer be subject to sin or death. They will be incorruptible and, hence, immortal (Aid To Bible Understanding). Bromiley says "At death, the individual will not escape from his body, but will feel it changed and glorified."

Following are the Biblical passages that support these notions:

1. 1 Corinthians 15:44—"It is sown a natural body; it is raised a spiritual body. There is a natural body, and there is a spiritual body." (The note on this passage says these bodies wil be similar to Christ's resurrected, glorified, physical body).
2. Philippians 3:21—"Who will change our vile body, that it may be fashioned like unto His glorified body..."
3. 1 Peter 1: 23—"Being born again, not of corruptible seed, but of incorruptible, by the word of God, which liveth and abideth for ever."
4. 1 Corinthians 15:52—"In a moment, in the twinkling of an eye, at the last trump: for the trumpet shall sound, and the dead shall be raised incorruptible, and we shall be changed."

WORSHIP

The Bible has much to say about how Jesus and God need to be worshipped. The Old Testament describes how Israel is supposed to worship in the tabernacle, temple and synagogues. (See, for example, Exodus, Leviticus, Numbers, Deuteronomy, 1 Kings, Ezra, Nehemiah, Psalms, Isaiah, 1 and 2 Chronicles).

The New Testament, especially, 1 Corinthians, Colossians, 1 Thessalonians, 1 Timothy, Titus, 1 Peter indicates how Christians following Christ's resurrection were to worship while on Earth.

If we want to get some idea as to how heavenly worship will be conducted, we need to rely heavily on the book of Revelation.

Assuming that the 24 elders in heaven provide other believers with a template for worship, Revelation 4:10-11 is enlightening. "The four and twenty elders fall down before Him that sat on the throne, and worship Him that liveth forever and ever, and cast their crowns before the throne, saying, Thou art worthy, O Lord, to receive glory and honour and power...."

Assuming that the angels and the elders and the four beasts (lion, calf, man, and eagle) are illustrative as to how the elect should worship (Revelation 7:11), let's see what it says: "They fell before the throne on their faces" and said that "blessing, glory, wisdom, thanksgiving, honor, power, and might should be accorded to God for ever and ever."

Revelation 7:14-15 describes how the saints which have endured the great tribulation will worship God: "Therefore are they before the throne of God and serve Him day and night in His temple.

Several hymns deal with the elect's worshipping activities in heaven. "All Hail The Power" (Perdone/Shrubs-Ole) contains these lyrics: "O that with yonder sacred throng, We at His feet may fall." "Come, Thou Almighty King" (de Giardini) alludes to singing, praise, prayer, blessing.

"His perfect salvation, His wonderful love. I'll shout with millions on high" are lyrics found in "He Hideth Me" (Crosby/Kirkpatrick). "All Hail The Power" Perronent/Holden states "that with yonder throng, we at his feet may fall; we'll join the everlasting throng," and states "that crown him....Lord of all."

Apparently, singing will be an important part of the elect's worshipping of God and Jesus in heaven. Revelation 13:1-3 refers to the people who got victory over the Anti Christ (martyrs) during the Great Tribulations and are now in heaven. They have "harps of gold" and they sing the song of Moses...and the song of the Lamb."

Several hymns deal with the subject of singing by believers when they get to heaven. The hymn, "Sweet By and By (Bennett/Webster) says: "We shall sing on that beautiful shore, The melodious songs of the blest." The hymn, "O Day Of Rest And Gladness" (Woods/Mason) contains these lyrics: "Bending before the throne, Sing Holy, Holy, Holy." The well/known and beloved hymn, "Amazing Grace" (Newton/Excell), says "When we've been there ten thousand years...we've no less days to sing God's praise, Than when we first begun." "When We All Get To Heaven"

FULL SALVATION

(Hewitt/Wilson) has these words in the chorus: "When we all get to heaven, We'll sing and shout the victory." The song, "Blessed Be The Name," opens with these words: "O for a thousand tongues to sing…The glories of my God and King" (Moorman/Moorman).

GOD IS WITH US ON EARTH

Matthew 21:3, where God is speaking to Joseph, Christ's earthly father, refers to this promise: "Behold, a virgin shall be with child, and shall bring forth a son, and they shall call his name, Emmanuel, which being interpreted is God with us." This passage is quite similar to that which is found in Isaiah 7:14, a pronouncement God made to the king of Judah, Ahaz. Thus, Emmanuel means "God with us."

Following are scriptures that provide support for this promise. In Genesis 28: 10-20, God told Jacob (later named Israel): "I am with thee..for I will not leave thee." When talking to Moses about dealing with Pharaoh, God said: "Certainly I will be with thee" (Exodus 3:12). God reassured Joshua as Israel prepared to retake the Holy Land by saying: "There shall not any man be able to stand before thee all the days of thy life: As I was with Moses, so I will be with thee: I will not fail thee nor forsake thee" (Joshua 1:5).

God gives the nation of Israel two general assurances that He will be with them during troublesome times. "God is in the midst of her; She shall not be moved: God shall help her, and that right early" (Psalm 46:5). Jeremiah 1:19 states: "And they shall fight against her; but they shall not prevail against thee, saith the Lord…"

When promising the prophet, Jeremiah, that no physical harm would befall him from an invading army, God said: "Be not afraid of their faces: for I am with thee to deliver thee, saith the Lord" (Jeremiah 1:8).

There are two passages in the New Testament that illustrate this promise from the stand-point of individual believers after the resurrection of Jesus Christ. Matthew 28:20 says "Teaching them to observe all things whatsoever I have commanded you: And I am with you alway, even unto the end of the world." (These are Jesus' words, after His resurrection, directed to the 11 apostles,

82

which gave them the charge to preach throughout the world, that is, the Great Commission). The note on verse 20 is most emphatic: "Matthew ends with the reassurance and empowering words of Him who came to Earth to be God with us."

Bromiley nicely summarizes the "God With Us" promise:

1. It distinguishes us from all other people (Exodus 33:16).
2. God enters into covenants with us (Deuteronomy 5:2).
3. God speaks to us (Hosea 22:4).
4. God walks with us (1 Kings 8:57).

There are a number of hymns that confirm that once a person is saved, Jesus will be with them during their sojourn on Earth:

1. "How Can I Be Lonely" (Lillenas/Lillenas): "How can I be lonely when I have Jesus only to be my companion and unfailing guide."
2. "Then I Met Jesus" (Carmony/Carmony): "He loved me and saved me, love without end, Now I am walking close by His side."
3. "Jesus Will Walk With Me" (Lillenas): "In joy or sorrow, today and tomorrow, I know He will walk with me."
4. "Jesus Loves Me" (Branbury): "Jesus loves me! He will stay close beside me all the way."
5. "Tis So Sweet To Trust In Jesus" (Stead/Kirkpatrick): "And I know that thou art with me to the end."
6. "Near The Cross" (Crosby/Doane): "Till my raptured soul shall find rest beyond the river, Help me walk from day to day."

THE RAPTURE

The word, "rapture," is not, as such, used in the Bible. The passage that describes this blessed event most fully is found in 1 Thessalonians 4:13-18 (The apostle Paul's words):

4:13: "But I would not have you to be ignorant, brethren, concerning them which are asleep that ye sorrow not, even as others which have no hope."

4:14: "For if we believe that Jesus died, and rose again, even do them also which sleep in Jesus will God bring with Him."

4:15: "For this we say unto you by the word of the Lord, that we which are alive and remain unto the coming of the Lord shall not prevent them which are asleep."

4:16: "For the Lord himself shall descend from heaven with a shout, with the voice of the archangel, and with the trump of God: And the dead in Christ shall rise first."

4:17: "Then we which are alive and remain shall be caught up together with them in the clouds, to meet the Lord in the air: and so shall we ever be with the Lord."

4:18: "Wherefore comfort one another with these words."

The Greek word for "caught" is "harpazo" which is translated "to snatch away." Thus, the rapture refers to the fact that saved people on earth and the saved, who have already physically died, will be removed from earth and those who have already physically died will be removed from earth "in the twinkling of an eye" and will be forever with the Lord.

When will this marvelous event, this rapture, occur? Most Biblical scholars believe that the rapture is associated with the "great tribulation," that is, the seven-year period on earth dominated by the worst tyrant the world will ever have, the Anti Christ. This person will control the whole world chiefly through a mechanism whereby no person will be able to buy or sell unless they have accepted the "mark" or name of the "beast" (the Anti Christ). Those who do not worship the Anti Christ will not be able to purchase food. Furthermore, many of these "non-compliants" (mainly believers) will be executed by the Anti Christ and adherents to him chiefly, as some Biblical experts believe, by the guillotine.

The second half of the great tribulation will be infinitely more chaotic and repressive than the first half. This will occur after the Anti Christ appears in the Jewish temple in Jerusalem and commits the "abomination of desolation" (see Matthew 24:15) by demanding that the world worship him as God (see Daniel 9:27). (The Anti-Christ will have entered into a seven-year peace pact with Israel before arriving in Jerusalem).

Theologians differ as to when the rapture will occur: at the beginning of the Great Tribulation, in its middle or at its end. Most of these experts believe that the elect will not have to endure the great tribulation, that is, the rapture will occur prior to the beginning of it. In support of their position, they refer to three instances in the Old Testament where believers were gotten "out of harm's way" so that they did not have to endure judgement. The Jews in Egypt were spared having their first borns killed when God inflicted this punishment on the first borns of the Egyptians. Noah and his wife and three sons and their wives did not have to endure the consequences of the flood. And Lot and his wife and daughters were spared the destruction of Sodom and Gomorrah because they had been instructed to leave.

How imminent is the rapture? Probably very close. Jesus, in His Olivet Discourse (mainly Matthew 24), gave some indications to his disciples as to when the rapture might occur. The astute reader will recognize that many of these signs of the end times are already occurring.

These include wars and rumors of wars, nations rising against nations, famines, pestilinces, earthquakes (in diverse places), Christians being persecuted, and the arrival of false prophets and false Christs. In Matthew 24:37-39, Jesus said "But as the days of Noe (Noah) were, so shall also the coming of the Son of Man be. For in those days that were before the flood, they were eating and drinking, marrying and giving in marriage, until the day that Noe entered the ark. And knew not until the flood came, and took them all away; so shall also the coming of the Son of Man be."

In providing an indication as to when His kingdom would occur, Jesus said (Luke 17:28-30): "Likewise also as it was in the days of Lot; they did eat, they drank, they planted, they builded, But the same day that Lot went out of Sodom, it rained fire and brimstone from heaven, and destroyed them all. Even thus shall it be in the day when the Son of Man is revealed."

There are several hymns that deal with the rapture. "After The Shadows" (Loes/Loes) contains these lyrics: "After the shadows, morning will greet us, Jesus will give us a wonderful peace, With our blest Saviour, glorious rapture." "Till my raptured soul shall find rest beyond the river" are lyrics in the hymn, "Near The Cross" (Crosby/Doane) "What If It Were Today?" (Morris/Morris) provides these lyrics: "Then shall the dead in Christ arise, Caught up to meet Him in the skies," ("What If It Were Today?").

REIGNING WITH JESUS DURING THE MILLENNIUM

The millennium is that thousand-year period when Jesus will come to earth to rule the world. And believers will rule with Him. This is stated in Revelation 20:6 regarding believers: "And shall reign with Him a thousand years." Special mention is made of the Christian martyrs who died in the Great Tribulation in Revelation 20:4: "And they lived and reigned with Christ a thousand years."

Below are some of the major aspects of the millennium:
1. The defeat of the armies of the Anti Christ will precede the start of the millennium.
2. Jesus will rule from his rightful throne in Jerusalem.
3. He will rule with a rod of iron (Revelation 2:27 and 12:5), that is, He will rule with strength (see note on Revelation 2:27).
4. The millennium will have unprecedented peace. Isaiah 2:4 is illustrative: "And He shall judge among the nations and rebuke many people: and they shall beat their swords into plow shares, and their spears into pruning hooks: Nation shall not lift up sword against nation, Neither shall they learn war any more. Isaiah 11:6 is pertinent, also: "The wolf also shall dwell with the Lamb, And the leopard shall lie

down with the kid, and the calf and the young lion and the fatling together."

5. At the outset of the millennium, Satan will be banished into the bottomless pit (Revelation 20:1-4). At the end of the thousand years, Satan will be "loosed a little season" (Revelation 20:3). At that time, he will "deceive the nations... to gather them together to battle." Satan's armies will surround Jerusalem, but God will summarily destroy them.
6. Despite the millennium being peaceful and ruled by Jesus Christ, some people will be so sin-ridden that they will buy into the deceitful strategies of Satan and will attempt to destroy the saints and the city, Jerusalem, where Jesus will be reigning.

There is an excellent video in which Pastor Mike Bickle explains what believers will be doing as they help Jesus reign on Earth during the thousand-year millennium. Bickle believes that already-resurrected saints in their glorified, spiritual bodies will rule over those saints who are still in their physical bodies and unsaved people. These ruling saints will serve in two capacities, as priests and judges, the same two that Jesus will have responsibility for. As priests, these saints will lead in worship in order to indicate the power of God. In acting in this capacity, we will serve as intercessors between people and God. As judges, we will decide innocence or guilt and the measure of punishment for transgressors. 1 Corinthians 6:2 says: "Do ye not know that the saints will judge the world?" (Revelation 20:4 mentions saints, their thrones and their rendering judgement). 1 Corinthians 6:3 says "Know ye not that we shall judge angels?"

During the millennium, the ruling saints will be involved with nations. We are instructed to teach all nations; Matthew 28:19 says "Go ye therefore, and teach all nations, baptizing them in the name of the Father, and of the Son, and of the Holy Ghost." According to Revelation 2:26, we will also judge the nations: "And he that overcometh, and keepeth my works unto the end, to him will I give power over the nations."

The saints will be charged with the rebuilding of nations — necessary due to their destruction during Armageddon and the events leading up to it. Amos 9:11, 14, in discussing Israel during the millennium, says: "And I will raise up his ruins, and I will build it as in the days of old; and they shall build the waste cities, and inhabit them."

In dealing with the nations, the elect will be charged with helping nations to make more effective use of their resources, especially regarding prudent land management. A reference to this responsibility is found in Amos 9:14:" And they shall plant vineyards, and drink the wine therefore; They shall also make gardens and eat the fruits of them."

The hymn, "He's Coming Back" (Boone/Boone), has a reference to the elect ruling with Jesus during the lillennium: "For a thousand years this earth will will have no temptation, and we'll reign down here with Jesus on the throne."

SECURITY OF THE BELIEVER

Can a believer lose his or her salvation? This is a pivotal question because if the answer is "yes," a Christian's faith and dependence on God's promises would be shaken to the core and many questions, as a result, will be raised by them:
1. What would I do that would cause me to lose my salvation?
2. Is there anything I need to do to avoid losing my salvation?
3. Did I not do the right thing or say the right words when I was supposedly born again?
4. Why does God hate me now? Did He ever love me?
5. What are the sins I might commit that would cause me to lose my salvation?
6. Are there any sins that I could commit that would not adversely affect my salvation?
7. If I did lose my salvation is there anything I could do to regain it?
8. If, as a Christian, I would lose my salvation, is there any other religion that I could embrace that would accept me and guarantee eternal life for me?

Theologians essentially take three positions regarding the loss of salvation. The two obious ones are "no" and "yes." But there is another one that has some support: Your sins did not cause you to lose your salvation because you were never saved in the first place. To start with, let's identify those hymns and their lyrics that undergird the "Once saved, always saved" position:

"Blessed Assurance" (Crosby/Knapp): "Blessed assurance, Jesus is mine."

"Praise Him! (Crosby/Allen): "He our rock, our hope of eternal salvation."

"Come To The Feast" (Homer/Ogden): "Praise God for full salvation."

"Glorious Things Of Thee Are Spoken" (Newton/ Haydn): "With salvation's wall surrounded, Thou mayst smile at all the foes,"

"He Hideth My Soul" (Crosby/Kirkpatrick): "His perfect salvation, His wonderful love."

"Saved, Saved!" (Scholfield/Scholfield): "He saves me from EVERY sin and harm, Secures my soul each day" (emphasis added)

Strong support for the notion that a Christian cannot lose his or her salvation is given by noted Biblical teacher, John MacArthur, in his book, "The Freedom And Power of Forgiveness." He bases his position on 1 John 1:9: "If we confess our sins, He is faithful and righteous to forgive us our sins and to cleanse us from ALL unrighteousness" (emphasis added).

MacArthur distinguished between judicial forgiveness and parental forgiveness. Whereas judicial forgiveness refers to being freed from the condemnation of a righteous and omniscient judge (God) whom we have wronged, parental forgiveness deals with the consequences of sin during our daily walk with a grieving and disappointed God, that is, God forgiving us and cleansing us of our sins (NOT taking away our salvation) after we have accepted Jesus Christ as our Lord and Savior.

While we do not lose our salvation when we sin, MacArthur believes that we need to daily confess our sins and to be remorseful and repentant as we do so. These bring about God's discipline, reproof and scourging; and they demonstrate God's love for you and confirms your relation to Him. According to Hebrews 12:6: "For whom the Lord loveth, He chasteneth, and scourges every son whom He receiveth"

MacArthur cites Psalm 32 to indicate the consequences of believers not confessing their sins: David said that when he didn't confess his sins, his "bones waxed cold, the Lord's "hand was heavy upon me" and "my moisture turned into the drought of summer." But when he "acknowledged my sins unto Thee;" "thou forgavest the iniquity of my sin." Note that this passage did not say anything about David's salvation being forfeited; don't forget that he committed some awful sins, such as, committing adultery with Bathsheba, engineering the death of her husband, Uriah the Hittite (one of David's most loyal and capable generals), and taking a census against God's will of the people which culminated in God sending a pestilence upon Israel which resulted in the death of 70,000 men.

The concept of being "sealed" is important in understanding the concept of the security of the believer. In the Old Testament, there are several examples of kings using their rings to seal documents. In the book of Esther, we note that King Ahasuerus (Xerxes) issued an edict allowing the Jews to be destroyed throughout the Persian empire (Esther 3:9). This order was sealed with the king's ring. This act of sealing meant that the order must be carried out; it could not be changed or dismissed (Esther 8:8). When the king learned about the plot to kill the Jews, his only option was to allow the Jews to defend themselves (Esther 8:11). This order was also sealed with the king's ring.

When King Nebuchadnezzar put Daniel in the lion's den, he had a stone placed over the opening "and the king sealed it with his own ring, and with the signet of his lords that the purpose MIGHT NOT BE CHANGED concerning Daniel" (Daniel 6:17, emphasis added).

There are several passages in the New Testament that employ the idea of being sealed and suggest the finality of a believer's salvation. Ephesians 1:13 states: "in whom also after that ye believed, ye were sealed with the Holy Spirit of promise." The note to this passage says that a "seal denoted ownership and SECURITY" (emphasis added).

John 6:27 says: "Labour not for the meat which perishes, but for that meat which endureth unto EVERLASTING LIFE, which the Son of Man shall give unto you: for him hath God the father SEALED" (emphasis added).

2 Timothy contains the following: "Nevertheless, the foundation of God standeth sure, having this seal. The Lord knoweth them that are His." (The note discussing seal in this passage says: "The church is owned and securely protected by God").

When Revelation discusses the plague of locusts on earth during the Great tribulation, the only human target will be "those men which have not the SEAL of God in their foreheads" (emphasis added). In other words, those individuals with God's seal will be protected (Revelation 9:4). Revelation 7:1-8 discusses the sealing of the 144,000 Jewish male witnesses (12,000 from each tribe) during the Great Tribulation. Verse 7:3 says: "Hurt not ....till we have sealed the servants of our God in their foreheads." This sealing was done in order to protect these 144,000 as they went throughout the world witnessing.

Besides the concept of sealing, the Bible offers additional evidence that Christians cannot lose their salvation;

1. "But now being made free from sin, and become servants to God, ye have your fruit unto holiness, and the end everlasting life" (Romans 6:22). This is not a conditional statement.

2. "For the wages of sin is death; but the gift of God is eternal life, through Jesus Christ our Lord" (Romans 6:23). This is not a conditional statement.

3. "For the law of the Spirit of life in Christ Jesus hath made me free from the law of sin and death" (Romans 8:2). This is not a conditional statement.
4. "And the blood of Jesus Christ His Son cleanseth from ALL sin" (1 John 1:7). (Emphasis added). This is not a conditional statement.
5. "Whosoever is born of God doth not commit sin; for His seed remaineth in him: and he cannot sin because he is born of God' (1 John 3:9). This is not a conditional statement.
6. "By the which we are sanctified through the offering of the body of Jesus Christ ONCE FOR ALL". (Hebrews 10:10). (Emphasis added). This is not a conditional statement.
7. "For by one offering he hath perfected FOR EVER them that are sanctified" (Hebrews 10:14). (Emphasis added). This is not a conditional statement.
8. "My sheep hear my voice, and I know them, and they follow me. And I give them eternal life; and they shall never perish, neither shall any man pluck them out of my hand" (John 10:28-29, Jesus' words). This is not a conditional statement.

There is a passage in the Bible (1 Corinthians 5:1-5) that addresses the issue of security of the believer. There was a man in the church at Corinth—according to the KJV Study Bible note he was a Christian—who was caught in fornication with this "father's wife" (the sinner's step mother). Such a relationship was clearly prohibited in Leviticus 18:8 and Deuteronomy 22:20.

The man was expelled from the congregation ("taken away from you," verse 2) for this sin so that he could be afflicted by Satan and would repent (verse 5). However, this man would not lose his salvation. Verse 5 says "to deliver such a one unto Satan for the destruction of the flesh that the spirit may be SAVED in the day of the Lord Jesus." The "day of the Lord Jesus" refers to when Christ returns (see note).

Noted pastor and theologian, Dr. Donald Grey Barnhouse in his book, The Invisible War, makes in the author's view the most compelling case for the belief that a Christian cannot lose his or her salvation:

"If there should come into the heart of an individual any concern as to whether he will be included in the divine plan, we may say to him that the general course of scripture authorizes us to believe that no such concern would ever arise in the heart of anyone who has not been chosen by God."

PROMISES ABOUT THE HOLY SPIRIT

Earlier, we discussed the Holy Spirit's role in salvation. Now, we will discuss the Spirit's role in the daily lives of believers.

There are a number of hymns that embrace some of the ideas about the Holy Spirit that will appear in the subsequent discussion about Him;

1. "The comforter has come!" "The Comforter Has Come" (Bottome/Kirkpatrick).
2. "No harm can befall, with my comforter near." (Montgomery/Koschat).
3. "Now the Spirit has control." "He Abides" (Buffum/Shanks).
4. "Holy Spirit, breathe on me, Take thou my heart, cleanse every part; Teach me in words of living flame what Christ would have me do." Breathe On Me" (Hatch/McKinney).
5. "Yes, this pow'r from heaven descended, With the sound of rushing wind." "Old Time Power" (Tillman/Tillman).
6. "Holy Spirit, Thou art welcome in this place." "Holy Spirit, Thou Art Welcome" (Hinn/Hinn).
7. "Holy Spirit, faithful guide, ever near the Christian's side." "Holy Spirit, Fathful Guide" (Wells/Wells).
8. "O send thy Spirit, Lord. Now unto me, That He may touch my eyes, And make me see." "Break Thou The Bread Of Life (Lathbury/Sherwin).
9. "Come, Holy Comforter, Thy sacred witness bear." "Come thou Almighty King" (de Giardini).
10. "Holy Ghost, With joy devine, Cheer this saddened heart of mine." "Holy Ghost With Light Devine" (Reed/Gottschalk).

When a person becomes born again, he or she is indwelt by the Holy Spirit. In Acts 1:5, Jesus said: "For John baptized with water, but ye shall be baptized with the Holy Ghost not many days hence." Indeed, 10 days later, at Pentecost this occurred with the apostles and others. Acts 2:14 says: "And when the day of Pentecost, was fully come, they were all with one accord in one place. And suddently there came a sound from heaven as of a mighty rushing wind...and they were all filled with the Holy Ghost..."

The reader will notice that the Pentecostal example talks about believers being FILLED with the Holy Ghost, that is, the Holy Spirit. One commentator, Bromiley, states that while all believers are endowed, that is, INDWELT by the Holy Spirit, some are more than just indwelt; they are FILLED with the Holy Spirit. Some examples include, of course, Jesus, at His baptism (Luke 3:22), Paul, Stephen (Acts 7:55), Philip, and Barnabas.

The Holy Spirit gives believers "fruits of the spirit." What are these? They are indicated in Galatians 5:22-23: love, joy, peace, long suffering, gentleness, goodness, fath, meekness, and temperance.

While fruits of the spirit help determine a believer's character, "gifts of the spirit" are given to them to make them more effective in carrying out their responsibilities, chiefly ministering. These tools are wisdom, knowledge, faith, healing, miracles, prophecy, discerning of spirits, divers kinds of tongues, and interpretation of tongues (1 Corinthians 12:8-10).

All believers have at least one or several of these gifts (1 Corinthians 12:7 and Ephesians 4:7), but no one person has all of them. These gifts are never to be used by believers for self profit; they are given to help them be more effective in their ministries.

Jesus, Himself, often used the word, "comforter," when indicating that the Holy Spirit would, indeed, come:

1. John 14:16: "And I will pray the Father, and He shall give you another comforter, that He may abide with you forever."
2. John 16:7: "Nevertheless, I tell you the truth; it is expedient for you that I go away: For if I go not away, the comforter will not come unto you; but if I depart, I will send Him unto you."
3. John 15:26: "But when the comforter is come, whom I will send unto you from the Father."

The Biblical passages, below, provide examples of how the comforter will assist believers:

1. John 14:26: "But the comforter, which is the Holy Ghost, whom the Father will send in My name, He shall TEACH you all things to your remembrance, whatsoever I have said unto you" (Jesus' words, emphasis added).

2. 2 Corinthians 1:4: "Who comforteth us in all our tribulation, that we may be able to COMFORT THEM WHICH ARE IN TROUBLE..." (Paul's words, emphasis added).

PEACE

Often referred to as "rest," Christians are guaranteed peace. Here are some of the hymns that provide this promise:

1. "Come unto me, I will give you rest." "Come Unto Me" (Jones/Jones).

2. "Till I heard a sweet voice saying, Make me your choice and I entered the haven of rest." "The Haven Of Rest" (Gilmour/Moore).

3. "His power can make you what you ought to be, Would you know the peace that comes by giving all?" "His Way With Thee" (Nusbaum/Nusbaum).

4. "Heavenly peace, divinest comfort, Perfect rest to me is promised." "All The Way My Savior Leads Me" (Crosby/Lowry).

5. "Master, the tempest is raging, The billows are tossing higher...peace be still, peace be still." "Master, The Tempest Is Raging" (Baker/Palmer).

6. "Come, all ye weary and oppressed, O come and I will give you rest." "Come Unto Me" (Hewitt/Milan).

7. "Out of the depths of ruin untold, Into the peace of the sheltering fold." "Jesus, I Come" (Sleeper/Stebbins).

8. "'Tis Jesus calls me on To perfect faith and love, To perfect hope, And peace and trust." "I Am Coming, Lord" (Hartsough/Hartsough).

9. "All fetters fall, And I shall find my peace." "Break Thou The Bread Of Life" (Lathbury/Sherwin).

We have already noticed that the millennium, Christ's reign on Earth, will be an unprecedented time of peace. Let's now see what our Lord and Savior had to say about peace (or rest) as applied to individual believers.

Probably the most relevant of Jesus' pronouncements on this subject is found in Matthew 11:28: "Come unto Me, all ye that labour and are heavy laden, and I will give you rest." The following verse, 11:29, is instructive, as well: "Take my yoke upon you and learn of me; for I am meek and lowly in heart: and ye shall find rest unto your souls."

Two of Christ's utterances suggest that peace will be an outcome of salvation. He said to the sinful woman who anointed His feet: "Thy faith hath saved thee; go in peace" (Luke 7:50). In Luke 8:48, He told the woman who had touched His garment and was made whole: "Daughter, be of good comfort: thy faith hath made thee whole, Go in peace."

Christ also used peace as a form of greeting. In Luke 24:36, after his resurrection, He said to His 10 disciples: "And as they spoke, Jesus himself stood in the midst of them, and saith unto them: Peace be unto you." The apostle, Paul, in the book of Philemon, also used peace similarly: "Grace to you, and peace from God our Father and the Lord Jesus Christ" (verse 3).

JOY

Believers can experience joy—a feeling that surpasses simple happiness or contentment. It rises above current circumstances because the joyful person focuses on God: His righteousness, His granting of salvation, mercy, and creation. Joy also occurs because believers know that God works out all things for the good of believers (Romans 8:28).

Believers can experience joy in times of trouble, even when persecuted and killed (Matthews 5:1-2).

The level of joy that Christians experience is in direct proportion to how close their walk is with God. (See Youngblood and Brand, Draper and English).

96

There are many hymns that acknowledge that joy in the life of believers is an important promise from God. Some of these are:

1. "It is joy unspeakable. I am saved from the awful guilt of sin." "Joy Unspeakable" (Warren/Warren).
2. "Raise your joys and triumphs high." "Christ The Lord Is Risen Today" (Wesley).
3. "With what joy I tell the story of the love that makes men free." "The Great Redeemer" (Foster/Beazley).
4. "They who believe on His name shall rejoice," "Jesus Is Calling" (Crosby/Stebbins).
5. "O, how our hearts beat high with joy, When 'ere we hear that glorious word." "Faith Of Our Fathers" (Faber/Hemy).
6. "Come, ye that love the Lord, and let our joys be known." "We're Marching To Zion" (Watts/Lowry).
7. "Take the name of Jesus with you. It will joy and comfort give you." "Take The Name Of Jesus With You" (Baxter/Doane).
8. "Since Jesus came into my heart, Floods of joy over my soul like the sea billows roll." "Since Jesus Came Into My Heart" (McDaniel/Gabriel).

HOPE

Believers are invested with hope; the note on Ephesians 2:8 says that "hope accompanies salvation."

By hope, we do not mean the ordinary idea we have of hope, that is, something desirable that we wish for and have SOME expectation that it might be granted. 1 Timothy 1:1 states: "Paul, an apostle of Jesus Christ by the commandment of God our Saviour, and Lord Jesus Christ, which is our hope." The note on this passage states that "hope expresses absolute certainty, not a mere wish." The note on Romans 5:5 ("And hope maketh not ashamed; because the love of God is shed abroad in our hearts by the Holy Ghost which is given unto us") states that hope is the blessed assurance of our future destiny." The note on 1 John 3:3 is also illustrative of the true nature of hope: "Not a mere wish, but unshakeable confidence concerning the future. The note on Romans 5:5 defines hope as the

"Christian's confidence that the purpose for which God created in him will be ultimately revealed."

There are a number of passages in the New Testament that nicely capture the above concept of hope and identify some of the specific outcomes believers can be assured will occur. Acts 24:15 says there will be a resurrection of the dead and we will not be ashamed. Titus 2:13 refers to the second coming of Jesus. 1 Peter 1:13 also ties in hope with the Lord's second coming.

Several hymns contain references to the promise of hope. "I've Anchored in Jesus" (Jones/Jones) has these lyrics: "Upon life's boundless ocean where billows roll, I've fixed my hope in Jesus, blest anchor of my soul." "My hope is built on nothing less than Jesus' blood and righteousness" are lyrics found in "The Sold Rock" (Mote/Bradbury).

Some Christian apologists believe that there is little difference, if any, among the concepts of hope, faith, and trust. While there is some merit in this position, there is one subtle, yet significant distinction: Faith and trust seem to be more a part of the salvation experience, whereas, hope appears to be more relevant after a person becomes born again.

THE ULTIMATE PROMISE

Revelation 21:1-2 discusses the "new heaven and the new earth" and the "holy city" which will all appear at the close of the millennium. Verse 21:3 states that God will dwell with men and they will be His people.

Verse 21:4, in my opinion, contains probably the most wonderful promise of the many that God has given His elect: "And God shall wipe away all tears from their eyes; and there shall be no more death, neither sorrow, nor crying, neither shall there be any more pain: for the former things are passed away." Verse 5 adds: "And He that sat upon the throne said, Behold, I make all things new." (Isaiah 25:6 and Revelation 7:17 also talk about God wiping away the tears of His people).

Look at what God is promising in the fourth verse of Revelation 21. Never again will we have to remember being afraid of dying, other events in our lives that caused us suffering and sorrow, the physical pain that we endured from illnesses and disease, and the mental pain that resulted from the deceit and betrayal of us by other people. Our thoughts will no longer be cluttered with these memories and we can then concentrate on what is truly important: loving God and Jesus, thanking them for what they have done for us, and worshipping them for all eternity.

Unfortunately, the unsaved will not be a participant in this glorious event. They will experience death for all eternity, that is, separation from God. They may express sorrow for their sins, but their pleas will fall on deaf ears. Any crying will also be ignored. Pain will occur from constant darkness and the flames that are apparently part of hell. And although the unsaved will no doubt shed copious amounts of tears, no one will be there to wipe them away.

Several hymns refer to Revelation 21:4, "No Night There" (Clement/Danks) contains these lyrics: "God shall wipe away all tears, There's no death, no pain, nor fears." The hymn, "Some Time We'll Understand" (Cornelius/McGranahan) states: "Some time with tearless eyes we'll see; yes, there, up there, we'll understand." "My Savior, First Of All" (Crosby/Sweney) comforts us with these words:" He will lead me where no tears will ever fall."

CHAPTER SIX

LIVING LIFE AS A CHRISTIAN

"In this world, ye shall have tribulation." (John 16:33)

M OST PEOPLE, INCLUDING CHRISTIANS, assume that once a person becomes saved, life will be a bed of roses. This may not be an illogical conclusion since a saved person is assured of salvation and this joyful situation is likely to permeate the Christian's life before he or she is taken home to be with the Lord.

It would be a mistake to think like this. In actuality, life even as a Christian, is likely to consist of a series of ups and downs. I have heard many ministers—in church pulpits, on radio and television, wherever—essentially say that as a Christian you CAN COUNT ON HAVING TROUBLES.

TROUBLES

What are some of these troubles? The "usual suspects" are the death of a spouse, spousal infidelity, divorce, death of a child, severe illness, financial difficulties, job loss, premature death of parents, and one of our own making—succumbing to temptations.

There are many hymns that demonstrate that Christians will experience difficulties. Some of these are:

1. "Tho' clouds may gather in the sky, and billows 'round me roll." "Sunlight" (Van DeVenter/Weeden).
2. "O sometimes the shadows are deep." "The Rock That Is Higher Than I" (Johnson/Fischer).
3. "Satan's snares may vex my soul from without and within." "I Want To See Him" (Cornelius/Cornelius).
4. "Jesus, Saviour, pilot me over life's temptations." "Jesus, Saviour, Pilot Me" (Hopper/Gould).
5. "When the woes of life o'er take me, Hopes deceive and fears annoy." "In The Cross Of Christ" (Bowring/Conkey).
6. "In seasons of distress and grief." "Sweet Hour Of Prayer" (Walford/Branbury).

The holy scriptures support the argument that Christians can expect to have to deal with difficulties after their conversion. Job 5:7 maintains that "man is born into trouble." The same sentiment is expressed in Job 14:1: "Man that is born of a woman is of few days and full of trouble." Jesus, himself, said in speaking to His disciples: "In the world, ye shall have tribulation" (John 16:33). Paul and Barnabas, when preaching at Iconium, warned that "We must through much tribulation enter into the kingdom of God" (Acts 14:22).

The apostle Paul's life as a Christian epitomizes the trials and tribulations that Christians often have to endure, especially if they are vigorous in preaching the good news of salvation. In 2 Corinthians 11:24-33, he alluded to receiving 39 stripes (five times) being beaten with rods (three times), stoned, shipwrecked (three times), being in water for a day and a half, being weary and in pain, hungry and thirsty, fasting, in cold and nakedness, being constantly in peril, and being imprisoned. (See Acts 16:16-33, Acts 28:33 and 2 Timothy 3:11).

One of the reasons why Christians are likely to experience trials and troubles is due to the assault on them by Satan because he reasons that he can get more mileage out of getting the elect to stumble than from non-Christians. Christians' sins will dissuade potential converts because they will think that "if that's the way Christians act, I don't want any part of it."

Donald Grey Barnhouse, the author of The Invisible War, provides important insight into the battle between Satan and Christians. The closer we walk with the Lord, the more we will be a target of Satan's hatred. Satan hates Christians because he knows that God will take away the original glories and functions granted by God to him and WILL GIVE THEM TO CHRISTIANS and they will be lifted higher than the angels and higher than the position originally given to Satan. If Satan can get Christians to sin, it would ruin God's newly-created life (see Genesis 1).

Barnhouse believes that this "invisible war" evolves around the extent to which a Christian will honor and glorify God or will live to achieve his or her own ends. Satan's desire is to denigrate the believer's spiritual life and his or her witness. Barnhouse postulates that Satan attacks us on three fronts: body (flesh), soul (temptations of the world), and spirit (Satan's malevolence).

Barnhouse maintains that there are limits to the weapons that Satan can employ to compromise our Christians walk. He is not omnipresent, that is, he cannot attack a number of Christians simulataneously. He is not omniscient; he does not know what is in the minds and hearts of Christians. And he does not know the future. Satan cannot indwell anyone who has been born again, meaning that we cannot be possessed by the Devil.

God permits Satan to attack us. Indeed, this is a recurrent theme throughout the book of Job. The purpose is to strengthen our walk with Him. God allowed Job to lose everything to show that Job would be vindicated in his steadfastness and would be a comfort to later Christians.

God puts limits on what Satan can do: Satan was allowed to do anything to Job except kill him.

God does not allow us to be tempted above what we can endure. All temptations are common to all of us. And He often provides us with a way of escape. (These three factors are found in 1 Corinthians 10:13).

Ephesians 6:11 indicates some strategies for dealing with Satan's attacks on us. The overall strategy is that we need to "put on the whole armor of God," that we may be able to stand against the wiles of the Devil. In that context, we are warned that we are not being assaulted by our earthly enemies but rather by "princi-palities, powers, rulers of the darkness of this world and spiritual wickedness in high places."

To fight Satan, we must depend on God's strength, his word and prayer (see note on Ephesians 6:17-18).

I don't want the reader to have the impression that the Christian life is a constant battle. Christ refutes this notion when He said: "Take my yoke upon you and learn of me...For my yoke is easy, and my burden is light" (Matthew 11:29-30).

There are a number of hymns that capture the essence of what we have just learned about a Christian's walk. Some of these are:

1. "Sunlight" (Van DeVenter/Weeden). "Tho clouds may gather in the sky, and billows round me roll, However, dark the works may be, I've sunlight in my soul."
2. "We'll Understand It Better" (C.A.T./Clark). "Temptation, hidden snares, often take us unawares."
3. "Jesus Will Walk With Me" (Lillenas/Lillenas). "In joy or sorrow, today and tomorrow, I know He will walk with me."
4. "In The Cross Of Christ (Bowring/Conkey). "In seasons of distress and grief, my soul has often found relief."
5. "I Need Thee Every Hour" (Hawks/Lowry). "I need thee every hour, in joy or pain."

What factors are important in determining how acceptable a believer's life is to God? While others may be important, I have seen the following identified as critical: steadfastness to the end in love of Christ, how have Jewish people and the nation of Israel been treated, and how capable have you been in handling your finances.

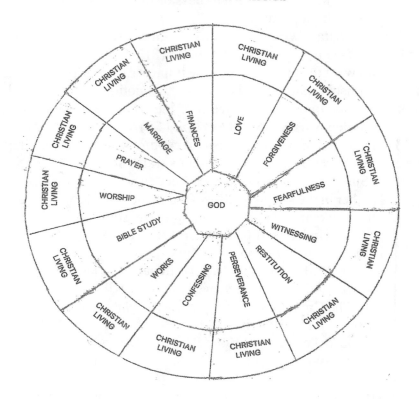

EXHIBIT 6.1
CHRISTIAN LIVING
GOD'S EXPECTATIONS OF BELIEVERS

Exhibit 6.1 depicts 13 expectations that God has laid out for Christians in their walk with him.

LOVE

As Christians, we are obligated to love God, our neighbors and, yes, even our enemies. Since it is through God's love that our sins have been forgiven, resulting in everlasting life for us, we will want to love our God in return. And this love cannot be lukewarm. Matthew 22:37 is illustrative: "Thou shalt love the Lord thy God with all thy heart, and with all thy soul and with all thy might." The note on this passage says that it addresses agape love, that is, a commandment of devotion that is directed by the will and is a duty.

Several Biblical passages demonstrate that Christians are required to love their neighbors. Jesus commands us: "Honor thy father and thy mother: and thou shalt love thy neighbor as thyself," (Matthew 19:19) In John 15:12, Jesus says to His apostles: "This is my commandment: That ye love one another as I have loved you." In John 15:13, Christ's words are also instructive: "Greater love hath no man than this: that a man lay down his life for his friends." An Old Testament passage (Leviticus 18:19) deals with the requirement that we are to love our neighbor: "Thou shalt not avenge, nor bear any grudge against the children of thy people, but thou shalt love thy neighbor as thyself. I am the Lord."

The type of love that should exist between neighbors is phileo love, that is, tender affection, such as that directed toward family members. It is used to portray God's love toward Jesus (John 5:20), for a believer (John 16:27) or for a disciple (John 20:12) (Brand, Draper and English).

Many Christians, quite frankly, have a great deal of reluctance to forgive their enemies, especially those that have significantly hurt them. However, this does not give us license to hate and plot against them. Jesus is adamant that we are to love our enemies: "Ye have heard that it has been said, Thou shalt love thy neighbor and hate thy enemy (see Leviticus 19:18), but I say unto you, love your enemies, bless them that curse you, do good to them that hate you, and pray for them which despitefully use you and persecute you" (Matthew 5:43-44).

A possible outcome of your loving your enemies is that they may be drawn to Jesus Christ because they perceive you, as a Christian, as being "different."

Love is one of the fruits of the spirit, along with joy, peace, long suffering, gentleness, goodness, and faith (Galatians 5:22).

The KJV Study Bible refers to 1 Corinthians, Chapter 13, as the "love chapter," after identifying what love isn't: speaking with tongues of men and angels, the gift of prophecy, and feeding the poor. This chapter (verse 13), ends thusly: "And now abideth faith, hope, charity, these three, but the greatest of these is charity," that is, love.

FORGIVENESS

Earlier, the concept of forgiveness as part of God's perspective in the granting of salvation to man was discussed. In this chapter, we will look at forgiveness from the viewpoint of the saved man or woman.

The scriptures are quite explicit: it is the obligation of Christians to forgive those who have harmed them in some way. The underpinning for this mandate is the idea that God forgave us for our sins, so we are obligated to reciprocate by forgiving those who have hurt us. Ephesians 4:32 says: "And be ye kind one to another, tenderhearted, forgiving one another, even as God for Christ's sake hath forgiven you."

Whatever rationales we use to not forgive, Jesus' words render them impotent. In Luke 6:37, He said "...forgive, and ye shall be forgiven." Other passages attributed to our Lord also mention a benefit that accrues to Christians who forgive. "For if ye forgive men their trespasses, your Heavenly Father will also forgive you (Matthew 6:14). Jesus makes a similar utterance in Mark 11:26: "But if ye do not forgive, neither will your Father which is in heaven forgive your trespasses."

There is a practical aspect from forgiving that accrues to Christians: They are able to rid themselves of the hold that the perpetrator of the harm has over them. They no longer have their daily lives consumed by bitterness, they can rid themselves of the shackles that bind them, move on and enjoy a greater level of contentment and joy in the Lord.

Many Christians, unfortunately, plot vengeance against their tormentors. The Bible warns against this mindset and, in fact, goes so far to say that it is not even necessary. Romans 12:19 says: "Dearly beloved, avenge not yourselves...for it is written, vengeance is mine; I will repay, saith the Lord." Hebrews 10:30 echoes Romans 12:19: "Vengeance belongeth unto Me, I will recompense saith the Lord."

An old Jewish adage indicates the folly of taking vengeance: "The man who plots vengeance had better dig two graves."

CHRISTIANS NEED TO BE FEARFUL

Christians need to have a fearful attitude toward God. We are not using the term, "fear," in its usual sense, that is, being afraid. The concept of fear used in the scriptures embodies the notion of reverence or respect. The note on Proverbs 1:7 says that "fear is a loving reverence for God that includes SUBMISSION to His lordship and to the commands of His word" (emphasis added).

Proverbs 1:7, itself, provides an important observation about fear: "The fear of the Lord is the beginning of knowledge." Knowledge in and of itself is important, but its real significance stems from the fact that from knowledge, wisdom—the ability to make appropriate and wise decisions—is achieved. The balance of Proverbs 1:7 adds: "But fools despise wisdom and instruction. Proverbs 16:16 elaborates: "How much better is it to get wisdom than gold."

WITNESSING

We have already seen that witnessing is an obligation for Christians. In fact, it could be argued that it is the most important responsibility that the elect have. Jesus' last words in Matthew to the 11 apostles were the "Great Commission" (Matthew 28:18-20), a reference to witnessing: "All power is given unto me. Go ye, therefore, and teach all nations, baptizing them in the name of the Father, and of the Son, and of the Holy Ghost: Teaching them to observe all things whatsoever I have commanded you: and lo, I am with you alway, even unto the end of the world."

Even though His words were directed to His apostles, they are relevant for all Christians. The note on Matthew 28:18-20 reads "Christ's Great Comission, though spoken to the eleven, was meant for the ENTIRE CHURCH, IN ALL AGES, UNTIL HE RETURNS" (Emphasis added)

This does not mean that all Christians need to become pastors or missionaries in overseas countries. But, they need to be constantly open to witnessing opportunities at work, at home, church, gatherings, commuter trains, stores, restaurants, in fact, anywhere.

It is important to understand that God may be instrumental in sending people your way who have exhibited receptivity to the Gospel. On the other hand, He may prompt you to approach someone who may be on the cusp of accepting Jesus as their Lord and Savior. Either way, you need to be aware of God's hand and be prepared to witness to them.

There are many stories recently coming out of the Middle East in which Muslims are experiencing dreams and visions which tell them to go to a certain place at a certain time. When they do this, they are approached by a Christian who leads them to accept Jesus. The apostle, Phillip, was told by the angel of the Lord to go to Gaza. Once there, the Holy Spirit prompted him to approach an Ethiopian eunuch who was receptive to the gospel. He was reading the book of Isaiah, essentially one of the most Messianic of all chapters in the Bible, chapter 53. Phillip witnessed to him, the eunuch accepted Christ and was baptized by Phillip that very day (Acts 8:26-40).

A Christian friend of mine went to a North African country on a missionary trip. While there, he followed the prompting of the Holy Spirit as to whom he should witness to. In every case, he was amazed because these individuals were not only hungry for the gospel but also could SPEAK ENGLISH; my friend could not speak Arabic.

We should always be willing to witness, but we should especially be excited about doing so at this time in history. Many Biblical scholars believe that we are in the "end times," the period leading up to the rise of the anti Christ, the great tribulation, and the second coming of Jesus Christ. Our objective when witnessing should be to bring as many people as possible to salvation before Jesus comes again. Matthew 9:37-38 suggests that there will be many people needing salvation, but there will be a dearth of individuals to witness to them: "The harvest truly is plenteous, but the labourers are few. Pray ye therefore the Lord of the harvest, that He will send labourers into His harvest."

The advent of mass media makes witnessing, today, able to reach more people. Newspapers, magazines, radio, television, computers (web sites, emails, blogs and social media), smart phones, and so on, are a boon for witnessing efforts. I think it is also a good idea to use tracts in our witnessing efforts. They should emphasize God's plan for salvation; they can be given personally to friends and acquaintances and be left in super markets, restaurants, shopping centers, sports arenas, etc.

What people are most likely to be receptive to your witnessing efforts? Two come to mind: those who are raising questions about salvation and those who are being overwhelmed and are desperate for help.

An overlooked aspect of our witnessing responsibility is the need to bring the good news of the gospel to our enemies. The following strategies are suggested to increase the level of success. Many of these are attributable to Mark Gabriel, a Moslem convert to Christianity (see my book, A Christian View Of The War Against Islam, pp. 135-136). Many of his recommendations are targeted to Moslems but also have applicability to all potential converts to Christianity:

1. Emphasize the gospels, especially the book of John.
2. Ask them about their understanding of the gospels.
3. Seek the Holy Spirit's assistance.
4. Be a friend. Invite them to your home, give of your time, help with their problems.
5. Explain what the Bible says about sin, forgiveness, and salvation.
6. Do not argue. Do not denigrate the potential convert's current religion or culture.
7. Be persistent, but be humble.
8. Tell them about Jesus.
9. Emphasize that salvation is a free gift from God and is not achieved through works.

There are many hymns that deal with the obligation of believers to witness. Here are some examples:

1. "The Name Of Jesus" (Martin/Lorene). "Jesus, let all saints proclaim its worthy praise forever."
2. "Redeemed" (Crosby/Kirkpatrick). "Redeemed—how I love to proclaim it."
3. "Turn Your Eyes Upon Jesus" (Lemmel/Lemmel). "Then go to the world that is dying, His perfect salvation to tell."
4. "Honey in The Rock" (Graves/Graves), "Then go out thro' the streets and byways, Preach the word to the many or few."
5. "Make Me A Blessing" (Wilson/Schuler). "Tell the sweet story of Christ and His love, Tell of His power to forgive."
6. "He Brought Me Out"(Zelley/Gilmore). "I'll sing of my salvation at home and abroad, Till many shall hear the truth and trust in God."
7. "The Regions Beyond" (Simpson/Simpson). "To the millions that never heard of His love, I must tell the sweet story of old."
8. "We've a Story To Tell" (Sterne/Nichol). "We've a story to tell to the nations and Christ's great kingdom shall come on earth."
9. "O Happy Day" (Doddridge/Rimbault). "Well may this glowing heart rejoice, And tell its rapture all abroad."

RESTITUTION

Restitution, in a Biblical context, has been defined as the "act of returning what has been wrongfully taken, or replacing what has been lost or damaged and the divine restoration of all things to their original order" (Brand, Draper and England). A synonym for restitution that is often used is "restoration."

Restitution is a concept that is mainly found in the Old Testament, particularly in the Laws of Property" (Exodus 22:1-15). If someone steals an ox or a sheep—and it is subsequently killed or sold—the guilty person is required to give the victim five oxen for each oxen stolen and four sheep for each stolen sheep.

Note that this restitution exceeds the original crime. A similar idea is found in Exodus 23:5: If a person causes another's vineyard to be eaten, he should make restitution of his best vineyard.

Restitution must be made if a person's fire causes a neighbor's harvested corn or corn in-the-field to be burned (Exodus 22:6). Exodus 22:10-12 requires that an individual replace a neighbor's ox, sheep or any other animal if he was asked to watch them and they were stolen.

The concept of restitution—and the need to recompense above the level of the original transgression—is dealt with in the New Testament (Luke 19:8) when Zaccheus, the chief tax collector ("publican"), said to Jesus: "Behold, Lord, the half of my goods I give to the poor; and if I have taken any thing from any man by false accusation, I restore him fourfold."

Acts 3:21 addresses the aspect of restitution that deals with the created order, that is, the universal renewal of the earth. This will only occur with the second coming of Jesus (see 1 Corinthians 15:25-28). I also feel that Isaiah 11:6-7 suggests this restored order, as well: "The wolf also shall dwell with the lamb, and the leopard shall lie down with the kid; and the calf and the young lion and the fatling together...And the cow and the bear shall feed; their young ones shall lie down together: and the lion shall eat straw like the ox." The note on this passage says: "The description is literal in that it portrays the transformation of nature that will occur..."

What are the implications of the notion of restitution for the believer? In short, you need to make an effort to make restitution to the people you have hurt through your past sins. This may not be easy to do: You may feel embarrassed or your behavior may have occurred so long ago that you may not know how to contact the aggrieved person. You may feel that what you did was justified because you were initially the aggrieved person. Since, as a saved individual, God has forgiven you for all of your sins, you may feel that you do not need to make restitution.

Despite these rationalizations, God expects you to do the right thing. Your efforts to make restitution may not always require that you make make a physical, probably, monetary, restitution. Sometimes, just admitting you were wrong and saying you are sorry may be sufficient.

Assuaging your guilt may be a benefit you will experience by making restitution. This effort will also give you the opportunity to identify yourself as a believer and open the door for you to witness to an unsaved person.

Many readers may have seen the movie, War Room. The ending provided a good example of restitution. The recently born-again husband/father offered to pay back to his employer the $19,000 he had stolen even though this was not a part of his original agreement to avoid legal prosecution (he also had lost his job).

There are a few hymns that address the concept of restitution. "Restore" (Chris August) offers these lyrics: "But God is a God Who knows how to heal. So just give it up to the Lord. And he will restore." Francis Augustus Blackmer's song, "Restitution Chorus," states: "For our God shall come with recompense, And his glory we shall see."

PERSEVERANCE

Perseverance refers to Christians maintaining their faith through their lives, especially through those trying times.

In this regard, Christians are urged to "endure to the end." Such endurance is indicative that an individual is saved. The note to Mark 13:13 says that perseverance is a sure indication of salvation and the note to Hebrews 3:14 states that "salvation is evidenced by continuing faith to the end." Paul refers to perseverance in 2 Timothy 4:7: "I have fought a good fight, I have finished my course, I have kept the faith."

In the New Testament, the writers were firmly convinced that those who truly committed themselves to Christ SHOULD persevere to the end because they had gained a new perspective and would not treat lightly this Biblical admonition (Hebrews 6:9-12 and Hebrews 10:39). They would finish the race because they would focus their attention on Jesus.

The passages dealing with perseverance appear to be directed to two groups of Christians. The first is to believers in general. Hebrews 3:14 reads: "For we are made partakers of Christ if we hold the beginning of our confidence steadfast to the end." Hebrews 6:11 is complementary; "And we desire that every one of you do shew the same diligence to the full assurance of hope to the end."

The second group are those Christians who are on earth during the Great Tribulation. Matthew 24:13 says: "But he that shall endure to the end, the same shall be saved." (Jesus' words). Mark 13:13 states: "And ye shall be hated of all men for my name's sake: but he that endureth to the end, the same shall be saved." (Jesus' words). In both of these passages, the end refers to the cessation of the Great Tribulation as brought about by Christ's second coming.

Below are three hymns that contain references to the need for Christians to persevere:

1. "O Jesus, I have promised to serve thee to the end." "O Jesus I Have Promised" (Merrill/Williams).
2. "Redeeming love has been my theme, And shall be till I die." "There Is A Fountain Filled With Blood" (Cowper/Mason).
3. "The work of faith will not be done, Till thou obtain the crown." "My Soul, Be On Thy Guard" (Heath/Mason).

CONFESS WITH THY MOUTH

As Christians, we are obligated to "confess Jesus with our mouths." What does this mean and why are we supposed to do this? We can get the answer to both these questions by examining the appropriate scriptures.

Matthew 10:32 says: "Whosoever therefore shall confess me before men, him will I confess also before my Father which is in heaven. Luke 12:8 makes a similar statement: "Also I say unto you, Whosoever shall confess Me before men, him shall the Son of Man also confess before the angels of God." Romans 10:9 is more explicit as to what this obligation consists of and what the end result is, that is, believing in your heart that God hath raised Jesus from the dead will result in your salvation. 1 John 4:15 says that for one who confesses that Jesus is the Son of God, God will dwell in him and he will dwell in God.

The note on Luke 12:8 concludes that when a person confesses that Jesus is the Messiah, Jesus acknowledges that this individual is His loyal follower.

In short, our willingness to confess, especially to others, that Jesus is our Lord and Savior is indicative of our salvation and, the author believes, it can be an important means to witness to non-believers.

There is one hymn that best captures the concept of confessing with thy mouth. "I Love To Tell The Story" (Hankey/Fischer) contains these lyrics: "I love to tell the story, 'Twill be my theme in glory, To tell the old, old story of Jesus and His love."

WORKS

We have noted earlier in this book that a person's works (deeds) will never result in that person being saved. The Biblical passage that most explicitly states this tenet is, of course, Ephesians 2:8-9: "For by grace are ye saved through faith; and that not of yourselves: it is the gift of God: Not of works, lest any man should boast."

AFTER a person becomes born again, works do become important, for several reasons. First, Christians are expected to work for the cause of Christ. Second, they give credence to the fact that we are Christians. Third, our works as believers are an important factor in determining the rewards we will receive on earth during the millennium and in heaven.

Let's identify the scriptures that support the notion that works are expected of Christians after they become born again. Interestingly, Ephesians 2:10 has this to say: "For we are His workmanship, created in Jesus Christ unto good works, which God hath before ordained that we should walk in them." Matthew 5:16 states "Let your light so shine before men, that they may see your good works, and glorify your Father which is in heaven" (Jesus' words).

Here are the scriptures that indicate that works confirm our salvation. James 2:14 says "What doth it profit, my brethren, though a man hath faith and have not works?" The note on this passage argues that genuine faith will produce good deeds. James 2:17 adds: "Even so faith if it not hath works, is dead..."

Following are the New Testament scriptures that support the notion that rewards are linked to a Christian's works. Matthew 16:27 says: "For the Son of Man is going to come in the glory of His Father with His angels; and with them recompense every man according to his deeds" (Jesus' words). 1 Corinthians 3:13-15 reveals that every person's works will be revealed. If a person's works survive, he or she will be rewarded, and if they are found to be lacking ("burnt"), he or she still will be saved. (More evidence supporting security of the believer).

J. Wallace and Keith Morrison ("Cold Case Christianity," internet) postulate that Jesus' parable of the talents (Matthew 25:14-30) is a clear indication that a Christian's rewards are a function of his works. In this parable, a man gives three of his servants, respectively, five, two and one talent—based on their abilities—while he was away in another country. Upon his return, the servant with five talents had earned an additional five talents, the servant with two talents had two more, but the servant with one talent earned nothing because he had buried it in the ground. The two servants who showed a return on the coins given them were told they would be made a "ruler over many things," whereas the man given the one talent was "cast into outer darkness."

Wallace and Morrison interpret this parable thusly: The parable indicates that believers will be rewarded according to their deeds and that those that do a lot with what God has given them will get a greater reward in heaven. They add: "If you squander what God has provided, don't be surprised to find that your reward is much less."

What types of works will be especially appreciated when God decides what kind of rewards will be given to believers? The Aid To Bible Understanding identifies the following: giving material assistance to or offering kindness to those in need or to those experiencing suffering or persecution, helping to make disciples, teaching fellow believers, and serving as an "overseer" in a Christian congregation (possibly refers to the position of elder).

The note on Matthew 25:31-46 is very specific as to the particular work that will be highly appreciated by God: The help given by Christians to Jews during the Great Tribulation. In focusing primarily on verses 41 and 46, the note says "Ultimately, how a person treats the Jewish people will reveal whether or not he is saved."

There are several hymns that, in general, proclaim that Christians need to be involved with performing works on behalf of Christ. The hymn, "Work For The Night Is Coming" (Walker/Mason) not only urges believers to work for the Lord but demands that they be relentless in their efforts: "Work for the night is coming, Work through the morning hours…Work through the sunny noon…under the sunset skies…fill brightest hours with labor."

"We'll Work Till Jesus Comes" (Mills/Miller) has these lyrics: "We'll work till Jesus comes..And we'll be gathered home." The following lyrics are contained in the hymn, "Ready" (S.E.L./Tillman): "Ready for service, lowly or great, ready to do His will."

When the contents of hymns are analyzed as to what specific kinds of works are expected, it is clear that witnessing is emphasized:

1. "Tell the sweet story of Christ and His love, Tell of his power to forgive." "Make Me A Blessing" (Wilson/Schuler).
2. "I love to tell the story, it did so much for me." "I Love To Tell The Story" (Hankey/Fischer).
3. "I'll sing of salvation at home and abroad, Till many shall hear the truth, And trust in God." "He Brought Me Out" (Zelley/Gilmour).
4. "More about Jesus would I know, More of His grace to others show." "More About Jesus" (Hewitt/Sweney).
5. "Pointing souls to Calvary, To the crimson flow." "O I Want To See Him" (Cornelius/Cornelius).
6. "To the millions that never heard of His love, I must tell the sweet story of old." "The Regions Beyond" (Simpson/Simpson).

BIBLE STUDY

You will want to grow as a Christian. The best way to do this is to develop the habit of reading and studying the Bible. It is a good idea to schedule a specific time each day to do so.

There are four major benefits that come from reading God's word. Believers will be sustained in times of need, they will be comforted in sorrow, they will be strengthened in times of weakness or temptation and sins, and they will become more in line with God's will.

The Bible is the inerrant word of God, so you can trust that what it says is true. Put your faith in what it says.

Many new Christians ponder over what translation of the Bible to use. While I prefer the King James version—it is the one I grew up with and memorized verses from—but the newer ones are also appropriate and probably use less formal language which may enhance their readability and understanding.

One of the most interesting developments in recent years is the publication of Bibles directed to various segments of the market. Some examples include editions for women, singles, men, teenagers, and young children. Some Bible versions emphasize a particular theme. The Bible focusing on prophecy comes to mind; all passages related to prophecy are presented in green.

Independent of what version you choose, there are four recommendations that will make your study more productive. First, select and use a Bible that has Jesus' words in red. Second, make sure that it contains explanatory notes; these will enhance and expedite your understanding of what you read. Third, consider using versions that contain such ancillaries as a subject index, outlines of books, maps, time lines, illustrations, diagrams, photos, and so on. Fourth, surround yourself with reference sources. (The author believes that those contained in this book's bibliography are a good starting point). These reference sources usually divide into two categories: concordances, which guide the user to what Biblical passages contain specific subjects (events, people, locations, etc.) and "encyclopedias" which discuss these events and various theological concepts.

Sunday school classes provide additional opportunities to study the Bible. So do small groups that may meet on a rotating basis at members' homes or in public places, such as, restaurants. The author and two of his friends met at Denny's once a week for breakfast where we would discuss various Biblical passages we had read and studied during the week.

There are a number of "game plans" available to help you in your studies. Some set up schedules for reading the entire Bible in 90 days, while others lay out a schedule over a longer period of time, usually a year. Besides these "read the entire Bible" scenarios, others may be more focused in that they deal with a recurring theme or topic, such as, prophecy, the life of Jesus, the minor prophets, the missionary journeys of Paul, the four synoptic gospels, the acts of the apostles, Biblical customs and culture, how the Old Testament points to Jesus, etc.

There are some standard "rules of thumb" that can be used to enhance your understanding of God's word. Identify the context (period of history, location, developments leading up to the event being discussed, cultural setting) of the passage you are reading. When speaking is involved, be sure you know who the speaker is and who the audience is. For example, it is helpful to know whether it was Jesus or the apostles speaking. Was the intended audience Jews or Gentiles, saved or unsaved? If you need clarification on a passage, consult the notes, if any, in the reference sources you use, or related passages that are indicated in some Bibles. Unless there is strong evidence to the contrary, accept literally what the scripture is saying. Finally, try to memorize some passages that are important for you to know, especially those helpful in your outreach to the unsaved or those that have a special meaning for you, such as, those that were instrumental in bringing about your salvation.

Don't be discouraged if you are unable to recall word-for-word Biblical passages that you are trying to memorize. (We can't all be like those people I have read about or seen on television who have memorized the entire Bible. This was either a gift from God or the person had a photographic memory!).

Here are some of the author's favorite passages which he has memorized (believe me, this was not accomplished in one day!):

1. John 3:16: "For God so loved the world, that He gave his only begotten Son, that whosoever believeth in Him should not perish but have everlasting life."
2. Acts 16:31: "Believe on the Lord Jesus Christ and thou shalt be saved, and thy house."
3. Ephesians 2:8-9 "For by grace are ye saved through faith; and that not of yourselves: it is the gift of God: Not of works, lest any man should boast."
4. Revelation 21:4: "And God shall wipe away all tears from their eyes; and there shall be no more death, neither sorrow nor crying, neither shall there be any more pain: For the former things are passed away."

5. Genesis 12:2-3: And I will make of thee a great nation, and I will bless thee, and make thy name great; for thou shalt be a blessing. And I will bless them that bless thee and curse him that curseth thee: and in thee shall all families of the earth be blessed.:

6. John 14:6: "Jesus saith unto him: I am the way, the truth and the life: no man cometh unto the Father but by me."

7. Psalm 23: "The Lord is my shepherd, I shall not want. He maketh me to lie down in green pastures: He leadeth me beside the still waters. He restoreth my soul: He leadeth me in the paths of righteousness for His name's sake. Yea, though I walk through the valley of the shadow of death, I will fear no evil: for thou art with me; Thy rod and thy staff they comfort me. Thou preparest a table before me in the presence of mine enemies: Thou anoinest my head with oil; my cup runneth over. Surely, goodness and mercy shall follow me all the days of my life: and I will dwell in the house of the Lord for ever."

8. Matthew 6:9-13: "Our Father which art in heaven, Hallowed be thy name. Thy kingdom come. Thy will be done in earth, as it is in heaven. Give us this day our daily bread. And forgive us our debts, as we forgive our debtors. And lead us not into temptation, but deliver us from evil: For thine is the kingdom, and the power, and the glory, for ever. Amen."

It is perfectly okay to "mark up" your Bible. The purpose of your studying the scriptures is to learn, that is, to acquire knowledge and convert it to wisdom, so make marginal notes, underline with a pencil, pen, or use a yellow marker. Many Christians have used these tools effectively in high school and/or college to great avail—so no reason not to use them when reading and studying the Bible.

There is one hymn that best captures the Christian's responsibility to study the Bible and the benefits of so doing. The hymn, "Jesus Loves Me" (Bradbury), cited in some hymnals as "The Favorite Hymn Of China," contains these lyrics: "Jesus loves me!, this I know, For the Bible tells me so."

WORSHIP

Christians need to regularly attend worship services. These include Sunday morning services and Sunday School. Many large churches will offer Sunday School for different demographic groups, such as, men, women, adults, junior high, high school, college students, singles, widows, and the elderly.

If your church offers Wednesday night services or Sunday night services, you should be also attending them on a regular basis.

It is absolutely imperative that your pastor ALWAYS preach the good news of the gospel, that is, we are all sinners and the only way to be forgiven for our sins is to accept Jesus Christ as our Lord and Savior. If your pastor does not preach this message consistently, worse, if he tells the congregation that there are many paths to salvation, start searching for another church where the pastor does preach the true gospel.

Be wary of churches that are getting swept up in the burgeoning ecumenical movement. This phenomenon is predicted in the Bible as occurring in the end times. It will culminate in a worldwide religion that is tightly integrated with a worldwide political power and will not be Christ centered. In fact, it will be the means whereby the Anti-Christ, that evil persecutor of Christians, will seize power.

Christ-centered churches will usually end their services with an altar call, where attendees are invited to the front and indicate their desire to accept Jesus Christ as their Lord and Savior. Or, they may want to rededicate their lives to Him or they may want to become a member of the congregation, or they may be asking for prayer.

Baptism is an important part of many worship services. Being baptized—the most acceptable method is total immersion, not sprinkling or dousing—allows the Christian to make a public declaration that he or she has accepted Jesus as Lord and Savior. But remember, as indicated in Chapter Four, that a believer does not have to be baptized to be saved.

In some congregations, there appears to be a schism developing over the type of music to be played and sung. Seniors usually favor the more traditional, older hymns, whereas younger ones seem to be gravitating toward today's popular Christian songs. It would appear that a compromise would be in order: half traditional and half modern.

In most churches, members are allowed to vote on major financial decisions. Many of these involve proposals for expansion of existing buildings or the construction of new ones. If these programs mean that the church's outreach efforts, such as, missionary work, would have to be reduced or eliminated, I would be inclined to vote no. This recommendation is based, in part, on my belief that we are in the end times and that gospel-loving churches should want to be a vigorous participant in the worldwide evangelical effort that will occur during this time.

Communion is an important part of many churches' worship services. Some offer it every week, whereas others may do so only once a year. An acceptable compromise, in my opinon, would be monthly on a regular basis, such as, the second Sunday of each month. All believers, whether members or visitors, should be allowed to participate in communion.

Following are some of the hymns that contain lyrics related to worship:
1. "O Worship The King" (Grant/Haydn). "O worship the King, all glorious above, O gratefully sing his power and love."
2. "Come, Thou Almighty King" (De Giardine). "Come Thou almighty King, Help us Thy name to sing, Help us to praise."
3. "I Am Thine, O Lord" (Crosby/Doane). "When I kneel in prayer, and with Thee, my God, I commune as friend with friend."
4. "My Faith Looks Up To Thee" (Palmer/Mason). "Now hear me while I pray, Take all my guilt away."
5. "O For A Thousand Tongues" (Wesley/Glaser). "O for a thousand tongues to sing, My great redeemer's praise."
6. "Praise Him! Praise Him!" (Crosby/Allen). "Praise Him! Praise Him! Tell of His excellent greatness; Praise Him, Praise Him, ever in joyful song."

PRAYER

Norbert Lieth (Midnight Call, January 2016) makes these observations about the prayer lives of Christians. We can pray either to Jesus or God. If we pray to Jesus, His Father, God, will also hear your prayers. We need to be praying in a quiet place, every day. We should be praying unceasingly, essentially not formal praying, but talking with Jesus and His father thoughout the day. Jesus (Matthew 6:7) urges us not to use "vain repetition, like the heathen do."

A humorous example of this mandate is found in 1 Kings 18:17-40 where 450 prophets of Baal engaged in a contest with the prophet, Elijah, to confirm who was the real God. The prophets used vain repetition ("O Baal, hear us"), leapt upon the altar and cut themselves to no avail: Baal was not able to bring fire down upon the altar, but Elijah was successful by uttering a SHORT prayer, ONE TIME. (The prophets of Baal tried for hours). As their efforts were failing, Elijah mocked them, thusly: "Cry aloud: for he is a god; either he is talking or he is pursuing, or he is in a journey, or peradventure he sleepeth and must be awakened" (verse 27).

What should be the components of the Christian's prayers? The author suggests the following:

1. Recognize the power, sovereignty, and love of God and Jesus.
2. Thank them for your salvation.
3. Thank God and Jesus for all aspects of your life: job, income, assets, children, spouse, friends, church, education, parents, siblings, etc.
4. Thank God and Jesus for our high standard of living, comforts, conveniences, ease of travel, health care, and so on.
5. Pray for the safety and salvation of your spouse, children, friends, acquaintances and those to whom you are witnessing.
6. Pray for your enemies and that they may be born again. Do not fall into the trap of using the "eye for an eye" and "tooth for a tooth" argument to justify not praying for them or praying for them to suffer harm. Romans 12:19 says "Vengeance is mine; I will repay saith the Lord." The note

on Psalms 5:10 says: "The psalmist knew that he who has been wronged is not to right that wrong by his own hand but leave redress to the Lord."

7. Pray for your pastor. Many pastors are under extreme pressure and, thus, deserve your prayerful support.
8. There is nothing wrong with asking the Lord for assistance or help.

In regard to this last recommendation, we know that God HEARS all prayers from Christians but we should not make the mistake that "hearing" means "granting". Below are the possible outcomes when we petition God for help:

1. Granting of the request in its entirety immediately.
2. Granting a part of the request immediately.
3. Granting the entire request or some of it later. (God's timing is always perfect).
4. Rejecting the Christian's plea. Remember that Paul prayed three times to God that He remove certain infirmities that were affecting the apostle, but God denied Paul's request.

Below are some hymns that contain lyrics that relate to the Christian's prayer life:

1. "Close To Thee" (Crosby/Vail). "Not for ease or worldly pleasure, Not for fame my prayer shall be."
2. "I Am Praying For You" (Cluff/Sankey). "Then pray that your Saviour may bring them to glory...I am praying, I'm praying for you."
3. "More Love To Thee" (Prentiss/Doane). "More love to Thee, O Christ, More love to Thee...This is all my prayer shall be."
4. "My Faith Looks Up To Thee" (Palmer/Mason). "Now hear me while I pray, Take all my guilt away."
5. "Neath The Old Olive Trees" (McKinney). "Jesus knelt on the ground, There He prayed 'Neath the old olive trees."
6. "Sweet Hour of Prayer" (Walford/Bradbury). "Sweet hour of prayer! Sweet hour of prayer! That calls me from a world of care."

7. "What A Friend" (Scriven/Converse). "What a privilege to carry everything to God in prayer."
8. "Whisper A Prayer" (Pate). "God answers prayer in the morning, God answers prayer at noon; God answers prayer in the evening."

MARRIAGE

This topic is important because marriage is approved and supported by God (see Hebrews 13.4 and 1 Corinthians 7:9) and the divorce rate for Christian marriages is no better than that for non-Christian marriages—an appalling 50 percent—resulting in horrific consequences for the children involved. The fact that Christ's first miracle—turning water into wine at a wedding—shows His respect for the institution of marriage (John 2:1-11).

The chief reason that God instituted marriage was for the proliferation of mankind (Genesis 1:27-28). "Marriage was designed to form a permanent bond between man and woman that they might be mutually helpful to each other" (Aid To Bible Understanding). In this regard, women were created to be a "help meet" for men (Genesis 2:18). After the fall of mankind through Satan's deviousness (Genesis 3), God laid out the consequences for both women and men in marriage. He told women that "in sorrow thou shalt bring forth children; and thy desire shall be to thy husband, and he shall rule over thee" (Genesis 3:16). This admonition is confirmed in the New Testament: "Neither was the man created for the woman, but the woman for the man" (1 Corinthians 11:9).

Men were told that "cursed is the ground for thy sake; in sorrow shalt thou eat of it all the days of thy life" (Genesis 3:17) and "in the sweat of thy face shalt thou eat bread" (Genesis 3:17, 19). In other words, husbands would have to work hard to provide for wives and children.

Aided and abetted by the feminist movement and such organizations as NOW, many wives, including Christian ones, have trouble with the notion that they are to be in submission to their husbands. They essentially ignore the mandate contained in Ephesians 5:22-24: "Wives, submit yourselves unto your own husband, as unto the

Lord. For the husband is the head of the wife, even as Christ is the head of the church. Therefore, as the church is subject unto Christ, so let the wives be to their own husbands in every thing."

As a corollary to the concept that wives need to be in submission to their husbands is the idea that they are also to respect them. Ephesians 5:33 says"…and the wife see that she reverence her husband."

Proverbs 31:10-31 is often called the passage of the "virtuous woman." Some of her recommended traits are she works with her hands, rises early to make meals, sews, is kind to the poor and needy, buys and sells, and supervises the household.

These are God's expectation for men:

1. He is to love his wife (Ephesians 5:25).
2. Wives are not to be mistreated by their husbands.
3. He is to provide his wife with food, clothing, and shelter (Aid To Bible Understanding).

The mention of the high divorce rate in America begs the question: What is God's view of divorce? In Mark 10:11-12, Christ said: "Whosoever shall put away his wife and marry another, committeth adultery against her. And if a woman shall put away her husband, and be married to another, she committeeth adultery." Jesus, in Mark 10:9, said: "What , therefore, God hath joined together, let not man put asunder." In other words, God takes a dim view of divorce. That said, He allows for divorce in the case of adultery ("fornication") (Matthew 19:8).

Let's not underestimate the severity of the consequences of adultery. Divorced spouses may suffer hurt, depression, anger, fear, and a reduced standard of living. In many cases, parents who live away from their children may be denied contact with them.

Children may suffer more than parents. Deep emotional scars may remain even after 10 years. They may blame themselves for the breakup, sense a lack of love, and may suffer from resentment, insecurity, and low self esteem.

The decision a person makes regarding whom to marry is second only to that of becoming saved. It is important not to hurry into marriage. The old saying, "Marry in haste, repent at leisure," is applicable. It is important to marry someone who is already a Christian (see 1 Corinthians 7:39). Do not assume that you will be able to lead the non-Christian to Jesus after marriage.

Pray that you will be making the right decision about a spouse. As you do so, be receptive to God's leading. I know two people, one a pastor, who said that God told them not to marry the person to whom they were engaged. Instead, they married women who were Christians who became their life-long companions.

If a Christian is married to a non-believer, the Bible says that they are "unevenly yoked" (2 Corinthians 6:14). The Bible recommends that the Christian spouse "should maintain the relationship in order to rear the children as believers and to win over the unbelieving spouse" (Brand, Draper and England).

FINANCES

Christians should not underestimate the importance of finaces in their walk with the Lord. We have already mentioned that some theologians believe that the way Christians handle their finances is an important way to determine how effective their walk is. Additionally, many Christian financial counselors believe that discord over financial matters permeate many marriages and are often a primary reason why many marriages, even in those where one or both spouses are saved, end up in disharmony, separation or even divorce.

There are a number of books, even workshops, available to guide Christians through the financial waters. There appear to be similar recommendations provided in these, some of which are Biblically based; others are just common sense.

Christians should be contributing a tenth (tithe) of their income to the local church they are attending. While the concept of tithing permeates the Old Testament (especially in Leviticus, Numbers and Deuteronomy) and often includes the donation of property (cattle, sheep, and harvests), The Aid To Bible Understanding maintains that at "no time were first-century Christians commanded to pay tithes." Apparently, the notion of tithing, however, became common place after that--perhaps based on the system that existed in Old Testament times—but more focused on monetary contributions instead of property donations.

A major question often asked is, do I tithe 10 percent of my gross or net income? The answer is gross income.

If you can afford to, there is no prohibition on your giving above that 10 percent figure to your local church. These gifts can be in money or kind (food, clothing, etc.). It is also appropriate to donate to other Christian or Jewish causes, the latter a result of God designating Jews as His "chosen people." His admonition to "bless" them (Genesis 12:3) and His exhortation to "pray for the peace of Jerusalem" is accompanied by the promise: "They shall prosper that love thee" (Psalm 122:6).

The scriptures suggest four groups that Christians might want to designate as priorities for their above-the-tithe giving. These are widows, the fatherless, the poor and strangers (or aliens or sojourners) (see 1 Timothy 5:3-16, Psalm 146:9, Deuteronomy 27:19, James 1:27, and Psalm 82:3-4). It should be noted that God loves aliens (Deuteronomy 10:19)—after all, the Jews had been aliens in Egypt for about 400 years—and the Jews passed special laws that provided aliens with food and clothing (Deuteronomy 24:19-20 and 26:12) (see Brand, Draper and England).

Do not feel put upon by your obligation to give to the Lord's work. 2 Corinthians 9:6 says: "He which soweth sparingly shall reap also sparingly; and he which soweth bountifully shall reap also bountifully." 2 Corinthians 9:7 adds that Christians should not give grudgingly, "or of necessity: for God loveth a cheerful giver."

Perhaps the best example of what a giver should be is found in Mark: 12-41-44. A poor widow put two mites into the collection plate—a mite being the least valuable coin at that time. Jesus commended her by saying that whereas the more affluent givers donated out of their abundance, "but she of her want did cast in all that she had, even all her living"

All Christians need to be conscientious savers. You need to do this to have enough money for retirement (a pension plan would be a great help), to pay cash for big-ticket items, and have a safety net in case of unexpected expenses. Most financial counselors feel that this safety net should be equal to at least six months' income. A

Christian financial counsellor I know has this rule of thumb: Tithe 10 percent, save ten percent and enjoy what's left.

It is imperative that you have a budget. You need to set spending limits on a monthly basis for food, utilities, gas, insurance, giving, clothing, newspaper and magazines, car payments and, yes, "fun" (movies, eating out, vacations) and so on. Do your best to stick to the guidelines. One suggestion: avoid making impulse purchases in stores. Arm yourself with a list of purchases to be made and stick to it! A recommendation for grocery shopping: Do a pantry audit before you make up your shopping list. Use items already on hand before purchasing new ones. This will minimize the possibility that items on hand will exceed the "use by" dates and have to be thrown out.

Keep track of what you are spending your money on. This discipline will enable you to see if you need to make budgetary adjustments—either up or down.

Check, on a monthly basis, your savings, checking and credit card statements to make sure that they reconcile correctly. This especially needs to be done to make sure that you are not the victim of identity theft or other unscrupulous means of stealing from you.

Christian financial planners are adamant that you not use credit. Their only exception is for a home mortgage. I am a little more flexible in believing that it is okay to borrow funds to acquire an automobile—but not for any other purchases. If you are not able to pay cash for an item, do not buy it!

The problem with credit is that it makes you beholden to your creditors, an undesirable situation. (Psalm 22:7 says: "And the borrower is servant to the lender").

THE SINNER'S PRAYER

If you want forgiveness for your sins and to be granted eternal salvation, the prayer below, or something similar, expressed with conviction, will be appropriate.

"Lord God, I know that I am a sinner. Please forgive me for my sins and grant me eternal salvation."

"I realize that forgiveness for me only comes from the shed blood of Jesus Christ on the cross. Thank you, Jesus, for your sacrifice. Thank you, Lord, for sending your son to the cross and raising him from the dead and his now being with you in heaven."

REFERENCES

AID TO BIBLE UNDERSTANDING, Watchtower Bible and Tract Society, New York, NY, 1971.

Kenneth Barker, General Editor, THE ZONDERVAN KJV STUDY BIBLE, Zondervan Publishing Company, Grand Rapids, MI, 2002.

Donald Grey Barnhouse, THE INVISIBLE WAR, Zondervan Publishing Company, Grand Rapids, MI, 1965.

Chad Brand, Charles Draper and Archie England, HOLMAN ILLUSTRATED BIBLE DICTIONARY, Holman Bible Publishers, Nashville, TN, 2003.

Geoffrey Bromiley, THE INTERNATIONAL STANDARD BIBLE ENCYCLOPEDIA, William B. Eerdmans Publishing Company, Grand Rapids , MI 1979.

Herbert Lockyer, Sr., Editor, ILLUSTRATED DICTIONARY OF THE BIBLE, Thomas Nelson Publishers, Nashville, TN, 1986.

Josh McDowell, GOD BREATHED: THE UNDENIABLE POWER AND RELIABILITY OF SCRIPTURE, Barbour Books, Uhrichsville, OH, 2015.

Orville, J. Nave, NAVE'S TOPICAL BIBLE, Thomas Nelson, Inc., Nashville, TN, 1979.

Earl Smith and John T. Benson, Editors, ALL-AMERICAN CHURCH HYMNAL, John T. Benson Publishing Company, Nashville, TN 1957.

William Smith, SMITH'S BIBLE DICTIONARY, Henderickson Publishers, Peabody, MA, 1993.

James Strong, THE NEW STRONG'S EXHAUSTIVE CONCORDANCE OF THE BIBLE, Thomas Nelson Publishers, Nashville, TN, 1996,

Merrill F. Unger, THE NEW UNGER'S BIBLE HANDBOOK, Moody Press, Chicago, IL, 1984.

Ronald F. Youngblood, General Editor, NELSON'S NEW ILLUSTRATED BIBLE DICTIONARY, Thomas Nelson Publishers, Nashville, TN, 1995.